Living the

Living the
Narrative Life

Stories as a Tool for
Meaning Making

Gian S. Pagnucci
Foreword by Lad Tobin

Boynton/Cook
HEINEMANN
Portsmouth, NH

Boynton/Cook Publishers, Inc.
A division of Reed Elsevier Inc.
361 Hanover Street
Portsmouth, NH 03801–3912
www.boyntoncook.com

Offices and agents throughout the world

The author and publisher wish to thank those who have generously given permission to reprint borrowed material:

Excerpt from "A Red Fox Again" from *Ancient Moves* by Franco Pagnucci. Copyright © 1998 by Franco Pagnucci. Reprinted by permission of Bur Oak Press, Inc.

"The Nose" by Gianfranco Pagnucci. Copyright by Gianfranco Pagnucci. Reprinted by permission of the author.

"Visions" from *Acorn*, 25.4 by Gian Pagnucci and Edel Reilly. Copyright © 2002 by Gian Pagnucci and Edel Reilly. Reprinted by permission of Bur Oak Press, Inc.

Library of Congress Cataloging-in-Publication Data
Pagnucci, Gian S.
    Living the narrative life : stories as a tool for meaning making / Gian S. Pagnucci.
        p. cm.
    Includes bibliographical references and index.
    ISBN 0-325-00623-7 (alk. paper)
    1. English language—Rhetoric—Study and teaching. 2. Report writing—Study and teaching
(Higher). 3. Narration (Rhetoric). 4. Storytelling. I. Title.

PE1404.P33 2004
808' .042'0711—dc22   2003028129

Editor: Jim Strickland
Production editor: Lynne Reed
Cover design: Joni Doherty
Typesetter: Kim Arney Mulcahy
Manufacturing: Steve Bernier

Printed in the United States of America on acid-free paper
08 07 06 05 04 DA 1 2 3 4 5

For Edel and Cormac,
the two most important stories of my life

Contents

PART FIVE

PART SIX

Foreword

I t's still hard for me to understand how telling stories ever got quite so controversial. I don't mean to be naïve here. I certainly understand why some people would prefer not to include narrative in their own academic writing and why those same people might prefer to read academic writing by others who share their sensibilities. Just because I like to write and read scholarship that includes or even relies on stories, just because I might choose to illustrate a point about the role of emotion in a productive teacher-student relationship by telling about the time my brother and I burned down our garage, doesn't mean I think everyone ought to share my commitment to narrative. In other words, I understand why some scholars avoid narrative and rely instead on textual analysis, the application of critical theory, or data from experimental studies.

What I can't understand, though, is why some of those scholars get so provoked when any of their colleagues or students don't share their point of view on this matter. Drop a personal story into an academic article and you're likely to stir up criticism, even if that story is clearly there to illustrate a point and even if the rest of the article clearly demonstrates intellectual rigor and sophistication. Again, I'm not trying to be disingenuous about this: I can understand the argument that for students to be empowered in the university they need to learn the conventions of academic discourse. But I don't see why we should ignore the power that narrative can also have to influence a reader, establish a credible ethos, or make a persuasive point. In fact, it makes no sense to tell our students that the use of personal narrative will limit their access to power and empowerment when they can clearly see the very powerful ways that stories are used in, say, advertising campaigns or political debates or religious sermons.

These are the sorts of thoughts that were stirred up for me when I read Gian Pagnucci's provocative *Living the Narrative Life: Stories as a Tool for*

Meaning Making. Exposing the flaws in the "hierarchy of forms" that dominates the academic world and that assumes abstract, highly theoretical writing is necessarily superior to clear and accessible narrative, Gian pushes us to wonder how we ever arrived at such dreary and illogical conclusions and why we continue to pass them along to the next generation of scholars. By mixing story, poem, essay, and scholarly research, Gian provides a model for a new kind of academic book. And by telling stories and by writing about the telling of stories, Gian seeks to make a place for pleasure, play, and personal connection in all forms of scholarly writing.

Those are ambitious goals and this is an ambitious book. In fact, what I like best about *Living the Narrative Life* is that Gian is willing to ask the sort of big questions that force us to re-think our most basic assumptions: why, he wonders, don't we ask literature students to respond to the short stories they are reading with short stories of their own? Why couldn't a dissertation be a novel or an academic book be a collage? What if we measured our success as teachers by asking whether something exciting happened each day?

The kind of provocative questions that Gian raises about teaching and scholarship generate serious thought but they also invite us to ask unconventional, even irreverent, questions about our own pedagogical methods and assumptions. Similarly, Gian's stories, like the ones about why collecting comic books was so important to him as a child or what it was like to walk through an Italian cemetery looking for his relatives' graves, made me want to tell my own stories in return. But beyond that, they made me want to continue the fight to promote and protect narrative, an almost endangered species in the academic world. And that, I think, is the response Gian is trying to produce in this book: though he advocates and employs playful and unorthodox methods, his goals are polemical and deadly serious, for Gian Pagnucci passionately believes that narrative is crucial not only for our writing and teaching but also for connection to our past, our future, and, most importantly, each other.

—Lad Tobin

Acknowledgments

Many people helped make this book a reality. I need to thank James Strickland right up front not only for having faith in my ability to write this book, but also for not giving up on me when I kept falling behind. His wise editing and even more forceful motivational speeches helped me through several moments of writing fatigue when I thought about giving up. In addition to Jim, I want to thank the many other Boynton/Cook Heinemann people who worked so hard on this book. These include, especially, Joni Doherty, who somehow read my mind as she designed the book's spectacular cover, Eric Chalek, Charlene Morris, and Lynne Reed.

I also need to thank David Schaafsma, my friend and onetime doctoral director. Dave not only taught me a great deal about narrative theory, but was also the first person I ever met who seemed to think about stories exactly the way I did. We both love and trust stories, and his support, guidance, and encouragement enabled me to carry this belief in narratives forward through my academic career.

My parents, Susan and Gianfranco Pagnucci, also were a great inspiration to me as I wrote this book. Together, they taught me to love good stories and to want to write and share those stories with others. My thinking about the importance of family stories has, naturally, been highly influenced by both my immediate and my extended family. The world just would not be the same for me without the stories I get from the Pagnucci and Reilly families.

I also want to thank my good friends David Henningsen and Steven Holland for taking me on more than one superheroic adventure whose influence has shaped this book. I hope I've been able to treasure a few stories here that would make them smile.

Many colleagues and close friends have influenced my thinking and ideas about narrative over the years. I'd like to acknowledge all these people, especially my frequent collaborators Nicholas Mauriello and William Macauley Jr.

My colleagues at Indiana University of Pennsylvania, particularly in IUP's Department of English and the Graduate Studies in Composition and TESOL Program, have greatly impacted me and helped me grow as a writer and a scholar in countless ways. I'd like to thank all those colleagues, especially Carole Bencich, David Downing, C. Mark Hurlbert, Donald McAndrew, Bennett Rafoth, Michael M. Williamson, and the much missed Patrick Hartwell. My interaction with a stellar group of colleagues from across a variety of academic fields in Project UNLOC (Understanding Narratives, Literacy, and Ourselves in Cyberspace) also served to help expand my notions of what narratives are and how we can use them.

Many, many students, through their writings and the stories of their lives, have taught me to appreciate the power of narratives. There are far too many to list them all, but especially important have been the graduate students who took my narrative theory and research seminars and those many doctoral students with whom I have presented and written collaboratively.

Finally, most importantly, I have to thank my wife for all her support and encouragement as I wrote this book. Edel Reilly is a natural storyteller whose enthusiasm for life never fails to excite and inspire me. Her driving spirit, much stronger than my own, helped me reach my own potential as an author. I would not have written this book if I had not had Edel in my life. And the goal and purpose of this book, to promote a better world through and for stories, also stems from Edel's influence because she is the one who gave me my wonderful son, Cormac, and he is the reason I am working so hard to save all these stories.

Introduction

Book Goals

This book is about choosing stories as a way of life. It explores the ideological ramifications of making such a choice and then offers a series of guides for how one might pursue this drive toward narrative. This book is filled with narratives, defenses of narrative ways of knowing, and explorations of the nature of narrative life. It is, on the whole, a kind of narrative credo, a conscious development of a narrative-based system of belief.

Why do we need a book about living the narrative life? A number of scholars have already argued that academic paradigms have shifted, allowing for a turn to narrative. Scholars like Cinthia Gannett (1999), Rubby Dhunpath (2000), and D. Jean Clandinin and F. Michael Connelley (1999), for instance, extol the importance and widening use of narrative research approaches, offering visions of a growing narrative movement. While I'm delighted and inspired by these scholars' work and feel hopeful about its implications for change, I remain, in the end, unconvinced that any real narrative turn has taken place. Instead, I argue that entrenched antinarrative views continue to make aligning oneself with the narrative camp a troubling prospect. The challenges that narrative teachers and scholars must face, challenges which continue to recur, have a very real ideological effect: they disempower and disenfranchise people dedicated to the study and creation of narrative scholarship. Pursuing narrative scholarship is thus a highly political choice, and a choice that often carries one to the margins of academe.

Unfortunately, the cost of resistance to narrative is extremely high. It means too many narrative-based studies are not conducted, too many narrative-focused books are not written, and too many storied ideas are not even whispered aloud. In the face of this antinarrative resistance, I offer this book as a challenge to the status quo. I wrote this book to lend support to those

1

who desire to do narrative research and to use narrative methods in their teaching. More importantly, this book examines and explores the highly charged nature of even making the decision to do this type of narrative research and teaching. I argue that narrative is an ideology and that believers in this ideology must struggle to come in from the margins and make their voices heard. That struggle begins with telling stories, stories of our families, our work, our teaching, our students, and, most importantly, ourselves. This book seeks to claim new space for narrative scholars and teachers, new room for them to tell the stories that matter.

It is my hope that this book will interest anyone sympathetic to narrative theories, particularly researchers, teachers, graduate faculty, and graduate students. The creative nature of this book will also make it a wonderful complement to research methodology courses. Finally, I designed this book to be a careful blending of story, poem, and theory in the hope that it will both inform and entertain a wide range of readers. Anyone who loves a good story should find something of value in this book, whether it is in reading the stories contained herein or in being motivated to start writing stories oneself.

This book is, in the final assessment, a guide to living the narrative life. That is not an easy life to live, but because it is a life rippled with the flow of stories, it is, in the end, the only life really worth living.

Book Structure

This book celebrates stories as a tool for meaning making. As such, I not only begin and end the book with narratives, but also tell stories throughout the theoretical essays. I have organized the book into six main sections. Each section begins with a short story I wrote to illustrate the main theme of the section. The story is then followed by a short poem that offers another interpretation and exploration of the theme and related issues. Finally, each section concludes with a theoretical essay, drawing from the relevant literature as well as a number of exemplary narratives. Taken together, the three elements of each section—story, poem, and essay—seek to unpack a variety of vital issues necessary for pursuing a narrative life. I have chosen to work in multiple genres, as well, to add weight to the argument that essayistic literacy is not the exclusive means by which one can create knowledge in the world, a view that is too often subscribed to within the ivory towers of academe.

I have also included two short interludes in the book, titled "Sharing Stories" and "Storied Wisdom." The first interlude is a collection of insights about the nature of narratives. I have culled these insights from years of conversations, classroom discussions, studied meditation, and random thinking. While the ideas are not wholly my own, I have reworked, modified, and orchestrated these concepts to offer a collage like interpretation of narrative theory. Narrative theory builds on a spirit of collaboration, taking as a central premise that we need to exchange stories with each other in order to make sense of our worlds. So I offer these interludes not as *my* definitive understanding of narrative theory, but rather as a kind of narrative heteroglossia, to borrow from Mikhail Bakhtin's work (1981). Bakhtin uses the term "heteroglossia" to describe the fluid, ever changing, chaotic nature of language, the way all words are infused with social, political, and cultural baggage, with ideological intention, with the stories of each speaker's life. The interludes in this book seek to capture this spirit of fluidity, motion, chaos, this mass of voices all talking together, like waves crashing into each other in Bakhtin's ocean of language, the ocean of heteroglossia. I am writing down these ideas here and now for consideration, but they have been formed over many years of dialogue and storied conversation.

The second interlude, "Storied Wisdom," is a pastiche of scholarly quotes reflecting on various dimensions of narrative theory, teaching, and research. The pastiche includes several ministories, also quoted from a variety of scholars and novelists (with any emphasis removed), as well as some of the simplest and most common statements about story that fill our everyday speech.

I have tried, in addition, to offer an artistic experience for readers with the two interludes. I argue, in Part Two, that narrative ideology celebrates art, and so I have tried to capture this spirit in the formatting of the interludes. Each interlude has been carefully formatted to guide readers through a specific aesthetic experience. For this reason, in "Storied Wisdom," I have dropped from a handful of quotations the authors' original textual emphasis where it would contrast too markedly with my own formatting choices for the interlude. I have also excerpted several texts to capture a given author's specific idea about narrative. In excerpting, I have worked to the best of my ability to remain true to each author's original spirit and intention. Full citations are included for those who wish to read the passages in their original contexts.

In creating these interludes, I have certainly been inspired by the work of Myka Vielstimmig (1999; 1999–2000), the collaborative authorial personality of my friends Kathleen Blake Yancey and Michael J. Spooner. I believe I offer less theorizing than they do, however. Instead, I have placed a variety of ideas and quotes into these collages to give them a chance to resonate in their own ways with readers. I hope, actually, that if nothing else, these interludes are fun to read and offer moments to rest from the more disconcerting stories and ideological arguments that engulf the rest of the book. Consider the interludes as places to pause and catch a breath.

Overview of Book Sections

Part One of the book tells my own story of coming to understand my need to live a narrative life. In my essay, "The Perils of the Narrative Life," I discuss a series of academic myths and false pretenses that help sustain antinarrative views in education. I try to show the hidden costs for all of us that stem from these obstructionist views.

Part Two of the book talks about the value of stories and the nature of narrative modes of thought. I use my essay, "Narrative Ideology" to explicate what I believe are the central tenets of a narrative view of the world.

Parts Three, Four, Five, and Six then discuss specific types of stories that I argue narrative ideologues should be writing, collecting, and studying. I begin with the need to tell one's own story, discussing, in "Telling Your Own Story," the narrative of my lifelong interest in comic books. I chose this decidedly unacademic topic to help challenge the many biases present in academia in regard to certain stories and genres. I seek to challenge the exclusion of any stories from the work of education.

Building from personal stories, I next move, in the fourth essay, "Telling Family Stories," to the need for us to begin directing more research efforts toward the collection and telling of those stories that shape us perhaps the most heavily, the stories of our own families. I argue that family stories are avoided in current research agendas and offer some discussion of what we might gain from working in this potentially rich area of research.

In my essay in Part Five, "Telling Work Legends," I discuss the nature of telling stories not only about teaching, the occupation of so many people interested in narrative thought, but also about other kinds of work, in this case, my specific experiences working as a technical writer. I use this essay to illustrate how the narratives of our work lives create belief systems that direct how we approach teaching. My story of working also serves as invitation for other people, both teachers and nonteachers, to tell their work legends.

I open Part Six with a series of "School Stories," narratives that are sometimes called "flash fiction" because the stories are extremely short vignettes—mere glimpses of the ongoing, multifaceted tales that make up our lives. I tell my small group of stories about educational situations in the spirit of the flash fiction recounted in Douglas Coupland's book, *Life After God* (1984), itself a lovely crystallizing of life's small moments of wisdom, sadness, laughter, and hope. The essay in Part Six, "Telling Stories with Students," picks up on this educational theme and tells a kind of dialogic story of my learning to teach and write with a young student. In this essay I try to tell a story of how teachers grow over time and how we might develop even more usefully as teachers when we learn to value the stories our students value. This section follows the path forged by other narrative teacher researchers.

Finally, I tell one last story, "Travelers' Tales," as a way to tie all the threads of the book back together, loosely, and emphasize, one more time, the central message of this book: that despite the ideological cost of pursuing narratives in our teaching and research, there is nothing more valuable for any of us than choosing to live a narrative life.

PART ONE

Awakening to the Narrative Life

It's a dark evening in late October, and I'm winding along Highway 286 in Western Pennsylvania. The BoDean's *Black and White* album (1991) is ringing out of my car's CD player and echoing off the hills that surround me. I'm thinking about the research writing class I've been teaching.

It's a boring class.

I turn up the music. And the heat.

It's not the students who are boring. It's the class. My class.

It starts to rain a little, then, and I switch on the wipers. At least that's how I'll remember it.

I try to figure out what's wrong with the class. I've set it up the right way. Starting with research questions. Letting the students pick their own topics. Getting into the library. Doing surveys and observations and interviews. It's all very scientific and professional. Exactly what the students need to get them ready for writing in their majors.

But what's exciting about it?

Those aren't even my words, actually, they're Mark's, and they take me to other thoughts, this time about curriculum planning. A group of us is trying to redesign the graduate program at our university. We try to set things up the right way. Some research courses. Some theory courses. But it's not easy work. People disagree. They start arguing. There's a little shouting. Angry words. Angry letters. Hurt feelings.

"What's exciting about this program?" Mark asked. It was a good question.

Mark even had an answer. He had a plan for the new program. That was the problem though. Everybody had a plan. Their own plan. But out here, on a dark country road, I remember. There was something special about Mark's plan. Something exciting. It was his starting point, the first course a student would take, a course he called "Stories of Self and Other."

When Mark presented his idea for the story course, someone said, "I worry about starting out with stories. We don't want people getting the idea that this is an easy graduate program."

"Better be careful," I thought. Then came the performance reviews and observations: I was new here. I didn't know if this was a place for stories. Some faculty members then said story writing wasn't real academic work. It was all good and fine to be creative, but that wasn't what students needed to learn to make it in college.

I listened to hear the way people talked about stories. What I heard made my head sink toward the floor.

Stories.

Such a basic part of life. Why didn't they understand?

Stories are how we think. How we talk. They form our governments, our religions, our cultures. They're how we fall in love. And how we fall out of it. Stories are what make us human.

Maybe.

Where are the stories in my research writing class? I look out at the darkness beyond my car window. Dave would be disappointed in me. And Dawn. And George. How could I forget about storytelling? Wasn't that what I had learned in graduate school? To trust in the power of stories? And now my first year of teaching wasn't even over, and I'd already forgotten. How? Why?

The road angles to the left, and I have to hit the brakes. All the roads in Western Pennsylvania seemed to be like this—sharp twists and turns, potholes, and loose gravel. I don't like this place. I miss my friends. I miss Madison. It is hard to talk about stories here.

I turn up the heat. Sam Llanas' voice floats out to me, and I drive along just listening to the music.

Why wasn't I using stories to teach writing? Stories were what excited me about writing. They were all I wrote. And it was writing stories that seemed to help me do my best thinking. And my best learning. The good teachers I knew, the ones I admired, they all used stories. Dave Schaafsma never told you anything without making it into a story. And Dawn Abt-Perkins could get kids to write stories when I thought they couldn't write anything at all. George Johnson told you a different story every time you met him, and some would nearly make you cry.

So where were the stories in my classes? I start thinking about the courses I've been teaching at IUP. Technical Writing. You *couldn't* write stories in a technical writing class. That was a class for writing memos and directions and reports. College Writing. You *couldn't* write many stories in there, either. That was a class for writing academic essays. And Research Writing. No room for stories there either. That was a class for writing those long research reports.

I smile a little. Then I turn up the music again. Sammy keeps singing to me, and I keep driving, and the mountains roll by on either side.

"You've got to get good student evaluations."

"The first year is the hardest."

"The first semester is the hardest."

"Document everything you do."

"You'll need a whole box of stuff for your promotion application."

"They don't give you much time for that."

"You should try to meet these people."

"You'll want to go to this workshop."

"You'll want to go to this party."

"You'll need this."

"You should do that."

I get a little scared.

I think back to my call to Edel late the night before.

"I can't do it. It's too hard."

"It's alright."

"They're always warning us about stuff."

"It's not so bad."

"I'm worried all the time. I was never worried like this before."

"You're just new. It'll be ok."

"Why didn't you come with me?"

"I can't yet."

"I miss you."

"I know."

I slow down a little, trying to focus on the music's echoing sound.

I think again about my research writing class. Along with their individual research studies, the students were doing one big project. We were researching the question: "How can IUP [our university] lower the cost of education for its students?" The class had voted on the research questions they wanted to study. It had seemed like a pretty good question to me. It wasn't too exciting, though.

I remember Kirk sitting in class a couple days before, reading *The Penn*, the IUP student newspaper. He had leaned back in his chair, pulled off his baseball cap, and run a hand through his hair.

"They just don't pay you guys enough, do they?" he said.

"What do you mean?" I asked him.

He spun the paper toward me. *Board of Regents Passes 4% Tuition Hike.*

"Guess not," I said. "Wish I was getting that bonus."

We both laughed.

The conversation struck me again, now, reverberating like the bass of the music. Of course the class had voted to study tuition costs. I remember looking out at their faces. They had looked serious. A little grim, even. It was hard paying for college. They all knew it.

And then we had gone on to something else.

How can IUP lower the cost of education for its students?

It really was a good question.

We'll write a proposal to lower tuition costs, I decide. *And then I'll get the president of the university to come in and hear the students read it. Even if I have to drag him.*

I smile, picturing my own moment of grandeur. Crusading for the common student. Saving the world. It's a nice story. My lights flash past a sign:

Indiana   10 miles

I should be having them write stories about getting an education. What it costs them to be here. What they had to give up. What they're hoping for. How much they're afraid to fail.

How can IUP lower the cost of education for its students?

The question is so basic. So personal. They asked it because the answer mattered.

Stories connect what we know to what we're trying to understand. They make things personal, give things meaning. They make things matter. That was the problem with my research class. I was making it an abstract exercise. Something impersonal and boring. I had cut out the stories.

Now I start remembering other things my students had said:

"Why is tuition going up?"

"Again."

"Where does all the money go?"

"How come we have to pay that activity fee? I never go to the gym."

"How come out-of-state students have to pay more? I haven't got any more money than anybody else."

"It's not fair."

"Why is it so hard to get financial aid? Don't they know my parents don't give me any money for school?"

"Why don't they pay student workers more?"

"I can't even get a student job."
"They just don't pay you guys enough, do they?"

——+——

Paying for college is not easy work. The students start arguing. Some people get angry and swear. They want help.

My students are hurting. Somebody needs to listen to them. The president really should hear what they have to say. And the key to my students' arguments is their stories:

"I can't afford this."
"I don't use that."
"I don't want that."
"I need your help."

They're trying to tell me about their lives, if I'll only listen. They'll write down their stories, if I'll only let them.

I drive up over a hill, and Indiana's lights splash out at me. I decide to make a few changes:

- We'll start writing more stories in my classes. *All* of my classes.
- I'll remember the things my friends have taught me.
- I'll worry less about what people think, and more about what's right.
- I'll get somebody important to come in and listen to what my students have to say.

It's a good list.

I drive down 2nd Street. The rain has stopped, but the music and the stories keep playing.

Almost

Someday, we might
Buy a winning ticket
Or write a hit song
Or find a treasure map

And get out of here,
To Koln Cathedral,
Or Windsor Castle,
Or the Himalayas,
Or just a Dublin pub.

But, for now,
Just tell the story again.
How you almost made it big,
How close you came,
How it was going to be.

Tell it.
I'll listen.
And the story will be.

The Perils of the Narrative Life

The sink in the basement was black from the soot of his hands. Vasco, my Great Grandfather, would sit on a stool and unlace his boots. Then he would strip to his t-shirt in the glow of the bulb hanging from the ceiling.

Above him, in the kitchen, he could hear his wife at the stove cooking a stew. He would eat hungrily, but his mouth would hold the taste of soot.

Vasco had come to America for a better life. But now he worked a 14 hour day deep down a mine shaft. Some days he ached to see the sunlight bouncing off the waves of the Mediterranean sea. To taste ripe figs again. To nap in the hot air of an Italian summer.

He laughed to himself, then. "Stupido," Vasco said, and rubbed his hands harder under the faucet. He was thinking like a child. There were no sea breezes here, no Italian figs. And no poverty. In Italy, they had nothing. Here, there was food and work and warm houses. A new school for the children.

Someday, he would go back to Italy, drive through the village in a big car. And then he would eat steak, not figs. Figs were for contadini, peasants. The money was good here. It was worth the long days underground.

Vasco wiped his hands on a worn towel and made his way slowly up the stairs to where his wife waited with a glass of wine.

"I don't see why I'm reading all this stuff about your great-grandfather. Are you proposing to do a study about him?" asked Dr. Richards.[1]

"No, no," said Brandon quickly.

---

1. This incident has been compiled based on a variety of real-world events. To protect the students and faculty involved, names, textual excerpts, and other key information have been greatly changed and modified. The characters are composites. While this is a work of fiction, this description is designed to be true to the experiences discussed.

I looked over at him. I could hear the slight note of panic in his voice.

"Well, this just doesn't seem to fit in here. There's this whole story about your great-grandfather moving to America. I don't really think that's relevant to a study about literacy trends in Pennsylvania," Dr. Richards continued.

"But I was just trying to set the context for where my interest in this study comes from," Brandon tried to explain.

"I agree with Dr. Richards," Dr. Xavier said. "You've *over* personalized things. This material really shouldn't be in your proposal. It might have been the genesis for your basic idea, but you need to ground the study in the relevant literature."

Brandon turned toward me, the panic in his voice now visible on his face. "Gian and I talked about this a lot. We thought it sets up the crucial nature of the study."

I cleared my throat and tried to save the day. "I told Brandon I thought he needed to start the proposal with this story about his great-grandfather because it highlights the historical context out of which literacy in Western Pennsylvania emerges. This pulls us into the study and helps us think about the kind of literacy stories Brandon might find as he collects his data."

"So you'll be looking for the literacy experiences of Italians, then? Or coal miners?" Dr. Richards asked. "That seems to be the subtext of the story."

"Well, it certainly could be," said Brandon. "Certainly, the mining experience is bound to be connected to the family histories of many of the people I'll be interviewing."

"It's likely," I said. "But it's also a way to see the set of values Brandon brings to the study. He's saying, 'I'm going in with this personal connection to the literacy of this place.'"

"Well, I'm not entirely sold on this approach. I'm really more interested in the viewpoint of your participants. I'm worried you're going to take away from their voices with all of this stuff about yourself," said Dr. Xavier.

I rubbed my eyes and shot Brandon a smile. "Well, OK," I said. "So that's one key concern. Why don't we keep moving, so we can work our way through the rest of the document?"

"Right," Brandon said. "Now that I'm completely frazzled, I think I'm ready to begin."

The Narrative Moment?

In the foreword to *The Personal Narrative*, Cinthia Gannett makes this optimistic claim about the narrative moment: "The number and variety of personal narratives are proliferating, not only as produced by students, but also by teachers, writers, and scholars" (1999, xiv). She goes on to cite an even more hopeful comment by Gillett and Beer about the burgeoning acceptance of narrative work: "Personal narratives from many sources, new and rediscovered, oral and written, now seem to abound. These narratives are part of a change in thinking which at last acknowledges that the autobiographies of 'ordinary' people can construct new knowledge about society" (xvi).

Rubby Dhunpath (2000) also speaks hopefully of the move toward narrative: "Biographies, life histories, and other modes of narrative research enjoy increasing popularity as an alternate genre" (543).

These scholars posit that we live in a time when narratives are gaining widespread acceptance. I wish that were true. But it's not.

The battle to legitimate narrative continues. A war metaphor may be a strong one to use, but it is necessary because the forces that work against the acceptance of narratives are subtle and persistent. Despite a number of scholarly volumes now currently available on narrative theory, the value of narrative research is frequently challenged. Dhunpath admits that narrative research's "status as a legitimate research methodology continues to be challenged by the positivist/empiricist tradition with its artificial dichotomy between qualitative and quantitative approaches to research" (543).

Those challenges come not only from traditional, conservative scholars, but also from more liberal scholars. Few dissertations, for example, are written in primarily narrative form, and few academic journals contain more than at most an occasional narrative essay or story. Even those that do publish narratives don't publish them in every issue. When narrative is featured in an academic journal, it's usually a special issue devoted to the question of whether or not teachers should ask their students to write personal essays in a composition class. And the few journals that do publish narratives are conspicuously absent from the lists of "leading publications" rated highly on tenure and promotion scholarship criteria at most universities. Look to *College Composition and Communication*, the foremost journal in composition, to find the academic, nonnarrative style in all its glory. And even when *College English* went so far as to offer two narrative-focused issues in a three-year time span (Hindman 2001; 2003), the issues did as much to challenge and dispute the value of narrative for academic work as they did to support it. *College English* viewed narrative as an issue to be debated, infrequently, and certainly not something to be celebrated.

But books and journals are not the most important territory over which we should be battling. The real place where narrative is most devalued is in the writing of dissertations: introduction, literature, methodology, data analysis, findings. Dissertations teach graduate students what really counts for academic writing. And as we teach these students to reify academic discourse, we turn them into teachers who celebrate such discourse above all others.

Do as we do, not as we say. We may claim to support personal narrative writing; we may even assign it as that first, "easy" paper in our courses. But the real writing, the academic research paper, is always waiting for when students are "advanced" enough to be ready to undertake it. The expository essay is the writing students need to do. And we ensure that our doctoral students believe that, too, because we've made them earn their union cards by writing the ultimate of all research papers: the dissertation.

So have things changed, have we experienced a narrative turn? The real answer is *no*.

The Challenges of Antinarrative Values

Unfortunately, this is more than a simple academic debate. The challenges that narrative teachers and scholars must face, challenges which continue to recur, have a very real ideological effect: they disempower and disenfranchise people dedicated to the study and creation of narrative scholarship. Pursuing narrative scholarship is thus a highly political choice, and a choice that often carries one to the margins of academe. I am not alone in making this claim. Noted narrative scholar David Schaafsma, in a 1999–2000 issue of *Works and Days*, recounts the real cost of his own choosing of a narrative life:

> In spite of the variety of interesting work in narrative inquiry and analysis being done in a variety of fields, and my own teaching of it as research methodology to teachers and doctoral students in a variety of disciplines, I had for years felt marginalized in certain ways within the ed schools where I had worked. "Stop telling stories," one senior professor advised me, in my first post-doc job. "And start writing about narrative." "Navel-gazing," another "mentor" labeled dimensions of my classroom stories. At my next stop my chair told me, "Stop writing stories, and stop writing with your students. Establish a strong individual scholarly niche." In my next stop, my present roost, they *finally* gave me tenure, appreciating the kind of narrative work I had done. (12, emphasis added)

To give one more vital illustration of this problem, in my own teaching, I have often heard comments, from both students *and* faculty, such as "Stories are too easy," "Are narratives *really* research?" "There's too much personal writing in this," and "But a dissertation can't be *just* a story."

Students hoping to pursue a narrative research agenda often have to fight faculty criticism to do so. Fortunately, some students are strong-willed enough to push for doing the kind of research they find meaningful, even in the face of opposition. Yet for those few who succeed in persuading a committee to support their efforts, there are many other students who early on abandon narrative lines of inquiry out of fear of the hardships such an approach will entail.

Of course, students can, and mostly do, find faculty support for their efforts even when the faculty may disagree about research methodology. But for students pursuing narrative research, passing a proposal defense does not resolve the issue. Human subjects review boards also resist, question, and hinder studies designed to pursue narrative investigations of the world. Both at my university and at the universities in which many of my graduate students teach, such review boards have often balked at and resisted the notion of studies that focus in any way on personal stories, particularly studies of one's own teaching. This is especially true when review board members are quantitative scientists, but it can also be true of some qualitative researchers. An ongoing objection is that the intimate relationship between the narrative researcher and his or her subjects cannot avoid coercive pressures. And of course, while coercion can be a problem for teachers who wish to study their own classrooms, what is overlooked is the cause and effect of this concern. While researchers might learn a great deal about teaching by studying and describing teaching settings over which they have a high degree of control, many of my students deliberately avoid designing such studies in order to bypass the hassle they would likely get from our review board. Action researchers' ongoing calls for teachers to study and write about their own classrooms (Clandinin and Connelley 1995; Goswami and Stillman 1987) cannot be met when teachers feel such research requires much greater effort than other researchers face because of the hindrance of human subjects review boards. This is not to say that boards never approve narrative or self-studies of classrooms, but only that the approval process for conducting such studies is far more difficult than for other research methods. What is important to note here, again, is that an antinarrative bias imposes a real limit on the research that actually takes place.

The Price of the Narrative Life

The costs of all these forms of resistance to narrative values are high. One cost is what we lose because of this resistance: too many studies never conducted or even proposed, too many books not written, too many ideas not even whispered aloud. There are also emotional costs—frustration, disappointment, fear, and anger—as narrative scholars face regular setbacks while trying to pursue their agendas. Finally, there is a human cost as well: the loss of stories. Academia's resistance to narrative causes stories to be blocked, removed, obscured, and untold in our classrooms and libraries. By arguing that stories are not fit for the academic world, academe often deprives students of the very thing that might help them make meaning of the things they are being taught (Egan 1986).

Fighting this antinarrative bias is, unfortunately, difficult. That makes it important for those who choose the narrative life to be conscious of the potentially negative ramifications of making that choice. Schaafsma crystallizes the dangers: "The real crux of the problem is this, that the academy does not truly value narrative as a way of knowing. I mean, things are changing in some places, and everyone is writing about it, but there's getting a job, and there's still tenure. It will mark you, in a way, put you on the outside, possibly" (1999–2000, 12).

Choosing to do narrative-based research can be a hard road. While the student in my opening scenario passed his proposal defense, it was not without difficulty. And the final dissertation defense is still an unknown outcome, with difficulties likely equal to the proportion of narrative elements he weaves into his final document. The case is no less intimidating for the scholar, particularly the developing scholar, who chooses to do narrative work. Publication venues are limited for narrative work. More importantly, tenure committees often frown on or belittle storied research. I have heard volumes criticized for being "too readable" or "too simplistic." Stories are often, incorrectly, called insignificant or easy.

Stories reach us in a form that naturally matches our basic modes for understanding the world (Bruner 1990; Schank 1990). But rather than being seen as a benefit of the form, this fact is instead commonly viewed as a limitation. Academia celebrates not clarity but obfuscation. We don't say what we mean. Bartholomae says we like muddied prose. In academia we prize abstraction and critical reflection. The piercing clarity of a story is too simplified for the hallowed halls of academia.

What I hope to do, then, is to help readers understand that choosing to live a narrative life comes at a price. Unfortunately, narrative is not an easy road, far from it. However, I also realize that for many of us, narratives are so powerful, we cannot choose any other sort of life. I mentioned to a friend that I once received an A on a paper that told a story of my early teaching experiences. He said, "People write so few stories in academic papers, when you do, they say, 'Wow, what a great thing. Thanks for taking the risk to share this story.' They don't understand that you don't have a choice. There's nothing else you could have done but tell a story. It's who you are."

Toubling Assumptions

There are a series of assumptions people make to criticize narratives. Most of these assumptions are themselves open to criticism. In this section, I'll work to unpack these assumptions and attempt to lay the groundwork for some basic support of narrative research and teaching approaches.

False Pretenses

I may have written a recipe for despair. I've said that the antinarrative bias in education is almost impossible to eradicate and that those sympathetic to narratives can't help but tell stories. So what are we to do? Well, let me suggest that we start by illuminating some of the false pretenses that support antinarrative beliefs.

The False Concept of the Field

The simplest place to start is with some discussion of people's almost naïve faith in the fields to which they belong. How do you recognize a field? The best place to spot it is in the waiting area of a major airport hub the day before a big disciplinary conference. Sit long enough in O'Hare Airport after Christmas and sooner or later, a few English professors will pass by, talking about postmodernism and their critical readings of some obscure eighteenth-century poem. They'll be on their way to the annual meeting of the Modern Language Association, and they'll be blissfully unaware of the many nervous graduate students also in that waiting area, anxiously rereading their vitae and wishing they had at least one more job interview to go to.

We want to believe that fields are built around a body of seminal works. We even have lists of these works that we give to graduate students to study for their comprehensive examinations. But this belief in a textual common ground is a fiction. We might find some books in common on these lists, but they vary from university to university. Most people haven't read all of those texts anyway, or else they read them so long ago that they only dimly remember the books' contents. We see this in catchphrases spoken or used in papers, a scholar's whole body of work boiled down to a title or code word. Copyright law's three hundred–word quotation limit also encourages people to discuss works at a shallow level, rather than looking at sources in greater detail. But even when we've read the same works, we know our readings of those works are often vastly different, inherently personalized as we filter them through our own sociocultural experiences.

The Russian theorist Mikhail Bakhtin explains that language is always shot through with ideology. Our language is colored both by us and by other people, and our language is shaped by the contexts, the sociocultural milieu in which the language is spoken. Thus when we talk together or read something, communicate in any way, Bakhtin says, we filter other people's utterances through our intentions and worldviews. We make language our own:

> As a living, socio-ideological concrete thing, as heteroglot opinion, language, for the individual consciousness, lies on the borderline between oneself and the other. The word in language is half someone else's. It becomes "one's own" only when the speaker populates it with his own intention, his own accent, when he appropriates the word, adapting it to his own semantic and expressive intention. (1981, 293)

Because language is so distinctly personal, our readings of texts are always individualized.

A field cannot, then, be built on shared meanings of texts. At best it can be built only on sharing particular texts. But deciding which texts to share is equally problematic. Consider E. D. Hirsch's attempt to do just that. Hirsch argued that what is needed for students' educational development is a shared cultural literacy, a common set of readings and books that everyone could be exposed to. But his list of great books, lacking in female and minority writers, was criticized as being insufficient and biased. So other, more inclusive lists were created. And, of course, before long, the lists were so big that no one could read all the books on them. So we were back where we started, with no common, shared literacy. For Hirsch's idea to work, for us to create a common literacy landscape, we would all have to agree on and then read the same set of books. But we can't agree because that would mean leaving some—actually most—of the books off the list.

Of course, even if we could agree on one list of great books that everyone should read, we would still face the task of actually getting people to read those books, a problem identified by novelist Jonathan Franzen, who confesses to fighting the lure of his television: "If you're a novelist and even *you* don't feel like reading, how can you expect anybody else to read your books?" (2003, 64, emphasis in the original).

So, while we might like to believe that there is a common field of English or composition, that simply isn't true. Some of your colleagues in the field, most of whom you've never met, have possibly read a few of the same books you have and know a few of the same authors and bits of jargon that you know. But that's about as far as the field's common ground actually extends. The real field of English or composition or physics exists mostly only within one's own department. That's right, the department where a person teaches. Of course, most of us aren't even on speaking terms with half of those people. Those of us who do travel to conferences mostly present to small groups of our friends and old classmates. Most people rarely bother to go to sessions that aren't given by keynote speakers. And even these "big names" would not be recognizable to the majority of people who teach the same subject we do. Our field doesn't exist. It's just a myth, a nice concept in theory, but not a real object. About all that really unites our field is the fact we all are English teachers and we all teach writing. Well, some people teach only literature. And some people teach only English as a second language. And so on. There is no field of English.

Yet despite this reality, the notion of the field is used to attack narrative research projects. "This isn't relevant to the field." "How can this one story inform the field?" "Who else in the field is looking at this?" Rather than constructing research for how it might be directly relevant to the people living it, we frame research for how it fits within a field that doesn't actually exist. This is not to say that research projects aren't designed with multiple purposes in mind, but the concept of the field is used to decide what is and isn't approved as genuine scholarship. Yet the field is a myth. The whole field will never look at a particular study. Many authors feel lucky when anyone reads their work.

If there is a field of English at all, then it is actually composed of those harried job seekers honing their MLA interview skills. What binds us together is our need for gainful employment. Our need for money is real. The rest of our common field is mostly imagined.

The Unacknowledged Hierarchy of Genre

The false reality of the field leads directly to another problem; our exclusionary ideas of what counts as legitimate scholarly work. One can return to Franzen, who, despite his own admission of a generally dwindling readership for books, still felt his own book *The Corrections* wouldn't interest the millions of readers in Oprah Winfrey's book club. Franzen said, essentially, that his book was too advanced for the readers of Oprah's book club:

> Among Franzen's trespasses was the observation that as a writer "solidly in the high-art literary tradition" he felt a bit squeamish about the Oprah's Book Club imprimatur; indeed, the embossed book-club seal of approval struck him as an unwelcome corporate logo, slapped carelessly onto the cover of a work he still regarded as "my creation." He was also intemperate enough to say that he found some Oprah picks "schmaltzy" and "one-dimensional." (Lehmann 2001)

While Franzen, to his credit, did explain later that he thought he had made a clear enough statement and was actually more troubled by the corporatization of the book industry than Oprah's readers, his remarks nevertheless alert us to the hierarchy of genre. In *How to Be Alone*, Franzen (2003) says he is a writer of "serious fiction." This implies that many other types of fiction, such as pieces of fiction chosen for Oprah's book club, are somehow not serious, that they are works of lesser account. But we needn't stop with concerns about different hierarchies of novels. Even Franzen's work would suffer at the hands of the elitism of the academy. Novels, even serious ones, are relegated to literature classes.

The work of the academy is done through expository essays, academic journals, and textbooks. There is little or no room in the academy for stories. I will rely on anecdotal proof here, but I believe that should suffice. In four years as an undergraduate at the University of Wisconsin, I worked my way through majors in international relations, engineering, computer science, economics, mathematics, and finally English and journalism. (Like many students, I took a while to figure out where I was headed!) In the process of all that coursework in all those different majors, I was never asked to read novels for any of my classes outside of English and history. If that isn't convincing, then all one need do is walk through a university bookstore at the start of the semester to scan shelf after shelf of required reading. Textbooks and essayist volumes abound, but novels or other volumes of stories are hard to find. Most university libraries don't even have large fiction collections. I recall once being told at a university library that if I was looking for fiction, I would be better off visiting the town's small public library. And even when one finds a novel chosen, the novel is usually a classic from the canon of "great" literature. The message is, if you are going to read fiction, which is a questionable activity at best, make sure it is at least "serious fiction." Everyday stories of people's lives do not suffice.

I'm confident that most readers of this volume, if they think back to their graduate school training (or consider it in the present), would have to admit that at the highest levels of the academy, the readings are decidedly free of stories. Mine were, except for those required by teachers who fell within the camp of narrative ideology. What is placed on the highest pedestal of all are not stories but rather theory, densely written works of abstract concepts. The academy prizes theory much more than it prizes stories. The reality of this is so self-evident we hardly even notice it.

As a graduate teacher myself, I have to admit that while I do use some books of stories in my classes, I never use only stories. I rely on more traditional academic material, journal articles, books of research articles, edited volumes of essays. In fact, whenever I have included a narrative work on a reading list, students responded by saying not only how much they enjoyed reading the narrative, but what a welcome change it was from their other required reading.

The trouble with this hierarchy, of course, is that it discourages people from writing narratives. Serious academic work is viewed as writing expository prose. People are not asked to write stories for undergraduate- or graduate-level work. Stories are viewed as light, simple, unimportant. Students see no models of stories to emulate in their scholarly work, and they get little encouragement to pursue knowledge in story form. Like all hierarchies, the hierarchy of genre works to keep some things at the top and other things at the bottom: stories are kept in the basement while theoretical texts reside in the penthouse. The selection of readings for students, one of the central guiding forces of students' educational lives, is clearly antinarrative in its orientation.

The Unreal Gap in the Literature

Another force that hurts the pursuit of narrative knowledge is the so-called gap in the literature. As virtually every doctoral student knows, a dissertation study is designed by reviewing the relevant literature on the topic of interest and finding an issue that has not been studied in detail, a research gap. The notion of the gap assumes, first off, that one can read all the relevant literature on a topic. Some ambitious graduate students may try to do this, especially those who read as an excuse to avoid actually working on writing their theses. But the notion of the gap is misleading. It assumes that, with countless databases, areas of study, conference proceedings, and websites, we can do what is virtually impossible—find and then read all the material on a topic.

Even if we could do all that reading, there's still the problem of the gap concept. What counts as a gap? What research is actually needed by the field? What has not been covered in a sufficient way? Certainly, we can look to calls for research, but these are often just one scholar's take on what needs to be researched next based on one study.

Of course, since the goal is to find a gap in the research, that's what students do. Most people are quite dutiful about performing the tasks they are assigned. So, students read the relevant literature and then say they have found a gap because that is what is required. Yet if we are honest, we have to admit that these gaps are, in many ways, simply manufactured for convenience. The notion of the gap is really a metaphor. Thinking about research literature as filled with gaps causes one to imagine knowledge as if it were a brick wall that is being built by a vast complement of colleagues. The wall is high and wide and has been built up for hundreds of years. But there are holes in the wall, gaps that need to be filled. Perhaps the base of the wall has even crumbled in spots, corroded by new, aggressive theoretical paints. When a doctoral student conducts a study and fills a gap, the student is acting as if that work places one more brick into the wall of knowledge.

By drawing out this metaphor, I hope I have illuminated its inherent fallacy. The notion of the gap assumes a kind of static knowledge set, one people slowly add to. It's quite similar to the banking model of education that Paulo Freire and Donaldo Macedo (1987) have critiqued so effectively. If, as educators, we have mostly learned that students are not empty vessels to be filled with knowledge, then why are we still trying to build a bank to hold the world's knowledge? The notion of a gap in the research pretends that knowledge is developed sequentially over time and that knowledge building is cumulative.

I should qualify, of course, that I don't think there is anything wrong with asking graduate students to do a review of the literature. If anything, I wish graduate students read even more than they do. My point, however, is that looking for a research gap is a kind of game. We conduct research in this way because that is what we have agreed with each other to do. And, of course, since the literature being reviewed is generally devoid of stories, the gaps people find are never missing stories. We get what we look for. If a person reads a hundred expository journal articles looking for a gap in the research and not one of these articles contains any stories, two things are certain: the student will find a gap so that he doesn't have to keep reading forever, and this gap will not contain a need for stories.

Am I stretching the argument, twisting things to suit my own agenda? Perhaps. But consider this. What if, instead of telling doctoral students, "Look for a gap in the research," we said, "Look for a story that needs to be told"? If we said, "Look for stories," that's what people would find. How we construct the research task heavily shapes the research outcome. Instead of trying to build a wall of knowledge, we could be asking people to add to the world's collection of stories. The point is, we could be aiming our research at narrative studies, but few people are because that's not what was done in the past. We have let choices become reality, myth become fact. And so we search for gaps and miss hearing stories.

The Misleading Limitations of Form

As a graduate faculty member for a large doctoral program, I've ended up reading a number of dissertations. Enlightening work? Yes. Thought-provoking? Yes. Pride-inducing? Yes. Exciting? Hell no.

Indiana University of Pennsylvania has some of the finest doctoral students in the country. And we are not alone. There are fantastic graduate students everywhere. To find them, all one has to do is ask their teachers. Yet, as wonderful as my own students are, so many of them have written dull dissertations. They couldn't help it. The form trapped them. As I stated before, nothing is more antinarrative than the traditional format of the dissertation: introduction, literature, methodology, data analysis, findings. Five chapters, all structured the same. Does a person really need a Ph.D. to write a five-paragraph essay?

Oh, this research story has a plot: Harried doctoral student reads and reads until, surprise, surprise, she finds a gap in the literature. Then she conducts her study as well as she can, preferably somewhere close by, at a low cost, and in a length of time much shorter than the ten years the perennial students have taken. With data in hand, she then writes something, fairly definitively, discussing what it all means. If she's lucky, we reward her with the title of doctor, congratulating her on becoming just like us. The trouble is, we've all heard that plot before.

Why did we ever decide that we wanted all dissertations to be structured the same way? Each semester I read three or four dissertations, depending on how many students happen to be defending at any given time and who is working on what projects with me. It doesn't take long doing this type of reading before a person is dying for anything fresh and out of the ordinary. As a reader, I crave stories, connections to what I am reading. Yet few dissertation studies are written or structured in a way to allow me to receive stories. So, instead, I read essayistic prose, as I know I'm supposed to.

I'm not saying there aren't exceptions to this. Joe Mackall wrote a fine dissertation called "Porch Stories" (1996), a short-story collection based on the research interviews he conducted while driving around Ohio. My own dissertation, "Cyberwriting: A Story of Teaching, Learning, and Co-authoring" (1995), written as a kind of novel, tells the story of my teaching creative writing to a teenage boy named Dustin. And while I certainly don't want everyone to write a novel just because I did, I also don't want everyone to write the same old five-chapter dissertation studies that have been written for hundreds of years. I should mention, as well, that just adding a sixth chapter to the template isn't much of a solution.

I hesitate to mention it, but there is one other problem with how we have structured our dissertation task. We ask people to write documents no one beyond the committee is likely to read. Sure, one or two industrious graduate students might eventually dig my dissertation out of Wisconsin's Memorial Library, but that's about as far as it will go. There was, in fact, a legend among UW graduate students that if a person stuck a twenty-dollar bill in her dissertation and came back in ten years' time, the twenty would still be marking the same page.

With so few readers, it seems odd that we feel compelled to make students write dissertations like everyone else. Perhaps we are afraid to ask for anything different, but if we are afraid, who is it we fear will read these startling new documents? I believe it would be a very good thing if more people actually sought out dissertations to read, even if they were just looking to see whether the writers were breaking the rules and slipping narratives inside those hallowed black covers.

I realize I'm making light of a serious situation, but I'm doing that because I find the reality of the situation actually quite sad. Given the countless hours people pour into writing a dissertation, it's a shame these volumes have so few readers. Even dissertations that get turned into books usually require radical trimming and editing. Why do we ask people to spend so much time writing documents we know no one would want to publish in that form anyway? Perhaps, if we pushed for dissertations that contained more stories, we might find more people who would actually want to read dissertations. Perhaps.

The Hidden Consequences of Critical Thinking

The academic world can be a cold place. Its campuses are big, its buildings are tall, and its classes grow larger and larger. And when students come to a university, they have to leave much of what they value behind: family, friends, beliefs, literacy patterns, value systems. This makes the place seem even colder. Teachers take pride in opening students' minds, working to help them consider their biases, their blind spots, their fears. The academy teaches the critical stance, the ability to look at things from a distance, to see hidden meanings and symbolic messages, to see how our thoughts are shaped and controlled by social and cultural forces. Reason, logic, and objectivity rule the day. Science and technology dominate the landscape.

For the most part, this is a good thing. We're never going to find a cure for cancer reading Shakespeare. And students do come to college with all sorts of limitations to their thinking and misguided beliefs. We have to work to build a world full of open-minded, tolerant citizens. It won't happen on its own. Critical thinking is a skill that needs to be taught.

Yet at the same time, if we take too much out, if we remove too much of students' original selves, they can never go back home. In his article "Literacy and Individual Consciousness," F. Niyi Akinnaso (2001) talks about the far-reaching changes that result from education. He points out, first off, "literacy alters the world we live in and the way we perceive and talk about the world" (140). Especially sensitive to this issue because he grew up in a basically pre-literate village in Nigeria during the 1940s, Akinnaso was one of the first in his village to develop written literacy, eventually even leaving the country to pursue a graduate education. In fact, Akinnaso attributes his move directly to his education: "Little did Father (or I, for that matter) realize that we were going to be permanently separated. For, as it turned out later, my quest for advanced literacy had to have a spatial dimension. . . . Moreover, the more I trained, the further away from home I went in search of a job" (142).

Akinnaso found that not only did education cause physical separation from his family, as he moved to locations closer to the schools he was attending, but it also caused mental separation: "The critical attitude that I began to develop in high school had grave consequences for my relationship with Father and others in the village. . . . I began to ask direct questions about the art of divination" (151), a form of religious practice in his village. Akinnaso says this caused his father to conclude that he was rebelling. It also brought Akinnaso into some conflict with the other villagers. Eventually, Akinnaso left his home village to take a teaching job in a nearby city. He observed, "I had developed certain habits which were not congruent with those prevalent in our tradition. I had developed a critical attitude and a sense of detachment or aloofness" (151–52).

It's clear from his article that Akinnaso highly prizes his education. He talks about his pleasures in reading Shakespeare and *The Arabian Nights*. But he also says he wished more of the villagers could have shared these pleasures with him. Akinnaso is keenly aware that his education has cut him off in some very real ways from his fellow villagers. Even more to the point, Akinnaso knows there is no way back: he cannot return to his village lifestyle because his thinking has been radically altered.

We work to educate students and, in fact, many times we succeed. But we have to be careful because we don't always consider, or even realize, the cost of that education. We consider the monetary cost, of course, and worry about the rising cost of tuition. But we forget that learning one thing may mean losing another. As we develop a critical mind, how much does that chip away at our emotional being? How much humanity has to be given up in order to gain reason? If someone had told Akinnaso, we'll teach you literacy, but that means you will never want to live in your village again, would he have agreed to be taught? Would his father have agreed to his education under such circumstances?

I'm not an advocate of ignorance. I believe in learning, both in school and throughout one's lifetime. But education is never simply about learning information: receiving an education also means receiving an ideology. Akinnaso learned to value the lifestyle of his teachers and to question the religion he had grown up with. In many ways, he was taught a Western view of the world, which is not surprising, given that he eventually studied at the University of California at Berkeley (142). Did he want to change in that way, to lose perhaps even his religion? Was it inevitable? Or did we change him without giving him a choice in the matter? We need to understand that when we teach people, we make decisions about how they will come to see the world, what their beliefs will be like. As academics we prize critical thinking because that's the way *we* think. There is some arrogance in assuming that's the way everyone should think.

I wonder, for instance, how different Akinnaso might have turned out had his schooling including reading and writing stories from his village life. What if the stories of Oodua and the Yoruba people (145) had been made a part of Akinnaso's education? I don't want to judge Akinnaso's life, say he is unhappy or that things didn't go well for him. That's Akinnaso's judgment to make. It does seem clear to me, however, that he and his education are the products of a particular set of values, values focused on critical thinking and objective reasoning. I've heard other such stories, such as those from teachers proud about helping students learn that a paper written using biblical sources was poorly argued and teachers delighted when students do enough reading to begin questioning previously held beliefs. That is education, but it is also an imposition of one set of values over another, a secular ideology over a religious one.

In *Letters for the Living* (1998), Michael Blitz and C. Mark Hurlbert try to create a classroom that resists the violence in our world:

> We try to make peace with the upheavals of the political world, the social environment, the ecology. Or we resist even the idea of making peace with the forces that, if they are not challenged and changed, threaten lives. The classroom is one important place to go to get past what has been done to us—and what we have done to others. It is the place where we can do work that adds needed things to our lives. (11)

I take their words as a caution against doing too much to my students. Some change is good, some is bad. I'm in no rush to push my students too far, and I worry when they start to sound like me. What I am most certain of is that every student brings his or her own stories to the classroom: what I try to do is make sure that the student leaves with those stories intact, perhaps even with those stories preserved in print.

In the remarkable book *Life of Pi*, by Yann Martel (2001), the protagonist of the story, Piscine (Pi) Molitor Patel, explores all sorts of religious views, becoming a Hindu, a Christian, and a Muslim. He passes no judgment upon these religions, instead choosing to see the value in all of them. His only criticism is with agnosticism because of its overreliance upon the god of reason:

> I can well imagine the atheist's last words: "White, white! L-L-Love! My God!"—and the deathbed leap of faith. Whereas the agnostic, if he stays true to his reasonable self, if he stays beholden to dry, yeast-less factuality,

might try to explain the warm light bathing him by saying, "Possibly a f-f-failing oxygenation of the b-b-brain," and, to the very end, lack imagination and miss the better story. (64)

While I am quite sympathetic to Pi's distaste for "dry, yeast-less factuality," I think his more important point is that religion, atheism, and agnosticism are all different kinds of stories, different kinds of ideologies for explaining the world. We have to remember that whether we teach critical thinking or narratives or writing, we are also always teaching ideology. We need to be careful to let our students decide what kind of story they will tell when their time comes. We shouldn't make their story conform to ours.

Radical Tales

This section has turned out much more aggressive than I had planned. But I suppose that shouldn't surprise me. It's frustrating, as the years go by, to see the bias against narratives persist. I hadn't meant to be a radical. Yet this book has turned out to be quite different from most academic works. It's full of stories, for one thing. And the stories are central to my arguments, rather than small anecdotes that can be dismissed. Ethnographers like to use vignettes, extremely short stories, to give readers a taste of a given culture. But while helpful, such stories are quite limited because of their length. And vignettes often fail to pack the emotional punch of more complex narratives. Van Maanen (1988) mentions, though, that ethnographic writing styles are slowly changing:

> Within the folds of anthropology and sociology certain changes are also afoot as a result of some of the newer, more experimental forms of ethnographic expression. Writers of realist tales . . . no longer treat observation alone with the same respect as previous generations did. Characterization of informants is more acceptable these days, as is a more personal writing style, with the author inclined to hide in third-party conventions. (125–26)

While these evolutions in ethnographic writing styles might give narrative supporters hope, at the same time, Van Maanen's words show us how far we still have to go.

In this book, I've tried to make *everything* personal. I've tried to show how stories from my life can illuminate the ideas I'm talking about, can help readers connect back to the stories in their own lives. But I've also done this so that the writing will help me learn as I go along. I've written this book as much for myself as for anyone else. That's another problem with the way we've designed our academic world. We've tried to be so distanced and critically reasoned that we've taken ourselves right out of the picture. We've made the academic experience so alienating that even we don't really belong, at least not as persons with all our personal idiosyncrasies. My hope, in the end, is that you will get as much out of reading this book as I have in writing it. And that you'll then be inspired to start writing down your own stories. Maybe part of my role, then, is cheering people on, the way Richard Meyer does in *Stories from the Heart* (1996).

While I may be cheering some people on, though, I also realize I have made some pretty harsh criticisms of the academy. I've attacked some of the things many academics hold as most valuable. I've criticized ideas like critical thinking and canonical literature. I worry that perhaps I've been too critical, too combative. But I also worry that if no one speaks up, there will never be enough room in the academy for all the good stories people have to tell. We'll always be so focused on teaching students how to write critical essays, so focused on getting them to write those precious research papers, that the narratives students actually need to tell in order to grow will never reach the page. I'm scared to criticize, but even more scared by what happens when we stay silent.

And then unexpected moments of humor have entered my writing. I've made a few jokes here and there. I certainly didn't set out to be a comedian. But the effectiveness of the jokes is less important to me than what I think they represent: emotion. From anger to laughter, narratives make emotional connections for us. Thus as I've written story after story, I've found my emotions being opened up onto the page. Again, this flies in the face of the cool reserve of the academy, the intellectual discourse on abstract issues of import. Here, I've tapped into things that seem to electrify my consciousness. Perhaps these are not the same issues that will electrify you, but I do believe stories have the power to find those connections for you.

Finally, I've even found myself experimenting with my writing, taking chances, trying things out to find new ways to approach these narrative topics. I have, for instance, included two wildly formatted interludes with loose collections of ideas about narrative. I hope these sections live up to the examples set by Myka Vielstimmig's "Petals on a Wet, Black Bough" (1999) and "From Hawaii to *Kairos*" (1999–2000) as well as the fragmentary quotes Tim O'Brien used in his book *In the Lake of the Woods* (1995). Vielstimmig, in particular, calls this a new kind of essay: "At the same time, it offers an aesthetic that gives writers permission to expose and explore the disconnects as they develop the plot of a given piece of writing—and permission to dramatize those disconnects, this process, in the concrete formatting choices they make (e.g., multiple fonts, shifting margins, etc.)" (1999, 90).

It feels very risky to try such things out. Perhaps these techniques won't connect with readers the way I hope. I don't know. What I do know is, I can't make sense of any of these ideas without telling stories. So that's what I've done, used stories to theorize about telling stories. I didn't realize that would make me a radical along the way. Still, just the notion of being a radical calls to mind a line from Richard Ohmann's book *English in America: A Radical View of the Profession*: "It seems to be characteristic of professions that they conceive their own advantage to be in the public interest" (1976, 209). Perhaps I'm doing the same thing with narrative, making what I believe appear to be in the public interest. It's a politically charged issue, figuring out what the goals of education should be. Since I've been advocating making stories a central part of those goals, I've clearly moved into the realm of ideology. I've been trying to position narrative in a positive light, as an answer to the limitations and failings of the academy. But that's still just one perspective, one way to view the problems and the solutions, one set of beliefs. Perhaps, then, following the narrative way of life always means being political, ideological, and radical. At least Ohmann is good company. Being a lone radical is far too hard and too risky.

Still, perhaps I'm just being grandiose. After all, this is an academic book. How risky is it really? How truly radical? How will it change the world? Think back to where we started, with Vasco, in the basement of his little house, washing up after a hard day's labor in the coal mines. Vasco risked everything to bring his family to a new world in the hopes of a better life. Compared with that, what sort of risk is it to make a few criticisms of the ivory towers of academia? Vasco risked a venture into the unknown, put his family's entire fortune at the mercy of traveling abroad. If it takes a radical ideology to make his story heard, to make all such stories heard, then so be it. Better to take a few chances than to leave Vasco toiling alone in a dim world. We need to hear his story. We need to work to make all such stories heard.

PART TWO

A Tennis Legend

Edward J. Bascom, 87, of Barnes, Wisconsin, died Thursday, August 21st, 2001, in his home. He was born July 18th, 1914, in Iron River, the son of Mike and Sheryl Bascom. Mr. Bascom was married to Margo Dodd of Platteville, Wisconsin. He is survived by his wife and two children, Jennifer and Tabitha. Mr. Bascom was a retired chemistry teacher. He loved to play tennis, served on the Barnes Community Council for 15 years, and was a dedicated member of the Wisconsin Synod Lutheran Church. He will be sadly missed by all who knew him. Friends will be received from 7 to 9 P.M. Tuesday at the Fisher Funeral Home in Cable. Funeral services will be held at 10:30 A.M. Wednesday with Chaplain Ronnie Spencer officiating. Interment to follow at St. Mary's Cemetery, Cable.

I sat quietly reading the obituary. Ed Bascom had died. My mother had sent me the obituary notice from the *Barnes Visitor's Guide*, which had apparently taken to running obituary notices in addition to its regular lineup of advertisements, "The Fisherman's Haul," and "Back Woods Recipes." My mother had jotted a note on the obituary: "He's the guy who took care of the tennis courts. He was still playing tennis at 87!"

I knew who Ed was. But I hadn't thought about him in years.

———

I was ten years old when my father taught my brother Rob and me how to play tennis. We learned to play on a couple of green asphalt courts in a small northern Wisconsin town called Barnes.

Those were great courts. There was this guy named Ed who used to take perfect care of them. He was the one who had originally petitioned the town council to build the courts. Ed watched over those courts all summer long. He swept the windblown sand off the courts, repaired holes in the nets, and even got the township to buy windbreaker netting for the west side of the courts' surrounding fence. And he vigilantly enforced the court rules written in red lettering on a large white sign bolted to the western court fence. Ed had come up with most of the rules himself, including the stupid one about not riding bikes on the tennis courts. He was always yelling at us for breaking that rule. Not that a bike could actually hurt a tennis court!

"You can't find better courts in the whole north woods," Clint Tannen used to say about the Barnes tennis courts. He drove an hour from his home in Superior just to use those courts.

———

Growing up playing tennis, you learn to appreciate good courts, especially ones that are well cared for and don't get constantly used by other people. That's why Dad always wanted to build a court on our lot. We had a wide flat area of grass down by the creek that he thought would make a great grass court.

I never thought a grass court would work that well. I was biased toward the asphalt courts I learned to play on. But Dad stood by the idea. "Grass is what they play on at Wimbledon," he would always say. "It's the royalty of the tennis world."

The thing is, though, a grass court requires constant care. You have to cut the grass real short and mow it all the time. And if it doesn't rain, you have to constantly water to keep the grass alive. And even a level area like ours would need to be bulldozed initially so that it would be smooth enough to play on. And then, if the ground shifted, the court surface would be thrown off, and you might have to bulldoze again.

I always figured the courts we played on in Barnes were good enough, but sometimes on summer nights I would lie in my bed and imagine getting up at seven A.M. to walk down the hill to our own private court to play a few sets while the air was still cool and the grass was dewy. There'd be no waiting in line to play, and afterwards we could walk back up to the house and have some of Mom's blueberry pancakes.

———

Once, when I was 16, I went to the courts to practice against the backboard. Dad had bought this orange wire ball cage, called a tennis hopper, off a television ad. It held maybe 30 balls, and I would keep serving them into the backboard until the cage was empty. Then all I had to do was walk around and drop the cage bottom onto the balls to pick them up.

The backboard was the one real weak spot of the Barnes courts. It was only about four feet across and three feet high with a white line painted across the middle. It was almost impossible to serve a ball into it and then catch the rebound with your backhand. The balls had a habit of hitting the board and then careening away at odd angles. Still, we didn't have a T.V. at the cottage, and there really wasn't much else to do. Plus I was always hoping that some beautiful girl might show up on her own looking for a tennis partner.

Of course, the only person who ever did show up was Ed. He'd drive up in his dusty blue Ford pickup, park it, leave the engine idling for a moment, and finally shut it off. Then he'd climb out, go to the back, and get out his toolbox. It was a big red metal box. I don't know why he needed all those tools, since the only repairs I ever saw him make were to the nets. But he always brought the toolbox with him.

That particular day I wasn't having any luck at all with the backboard, so I got it into my head to complain to Ed about it. Surely Ed would see that the cheap small backboard should be replaced with a full wall panel for practicing.

"Nothing doing," Ed told me. "That backboard is the best way to improve your game. It requires pinpoint accuracy."

"Oh, come on, Ed. Rob and I are about the only ones who use it because it's so damn hard to hit into. I've never seen anyone get more than about four returns into it."

"There's nothing wrong with the backboard. I put that up myself five years ago, and I'm not about to waste the town council's money on a new one."

Cheap, cheap, cheap, I thought. But I could see I wasn't getting any-where, so I went back to snagging balls with the hopper. After that, I took a few more practice serves and decided it was time to head for home. I gathered up my stuff and started walking to where I'd left my bike.

Ed was fooling with a hinge on one of the metal gates, trying to get it to stop squeaking. So I walked over to him to say good-bye.

"Say, Ed," I asked, when I got up to him. "Why do you spend so much time taking care of these courts anyway? I mean, they really are great courts. We love to play here."

Ed paused for a moment, then lowered his can of WD-40 to the ground and wiped his brow with a rag.

"My son, Danny, loved to play tennis. He was a star of his high school team. The only kid ever to make it to state from Hayward."

"When's he coming to visit you? Maybe I could play a few sets with him."

"He passed away," said Ed. "He was shot in a rice field in Vietnam."

"Oh. I'm sorry," I said. I didn't know much about the Vietnam War. I'd heard of it. But we never seemed to get to that topic in history. It took too long to cover the Revolutionary War.

"Danny loved tennis. He had a scholarship to Edgewood to play tennis in college. But he got drafted before he ever made it into school. And then he never came back."

"Oh," I said again.

"I got the council to build this court in memory of him."

"Wow, that's great," I said. "Maybe you should put up a plaque about him."

"Nah," said Ed with a smile. "The courts are enough."

"Yeah, but," I paused and thought carefully for a moment. "Wouldn't you like people to know a little about Danny's story?"

"No."

"Why not?" I asked. I thought a plaque was a great idea, personally. Dad was always stopping at those plaques along the highways that mark historical sites.

"Just don't want to," he said.

"But then people would think about your son, when they read his story," I said.

"Stories don't last," said Ed. "My son's gone. There's just the courts now. That's enough."

———

I set the obituary down on my desk. Now Ed and Danny were both gone. And Ed never had put up a plaque. *Maybe they'll rename the courts after Ed,* I thought.

I spent a few minutes debating about trying to find a last-minute airline ticket so I could go out to the funeral. I imagined Ed laid out in his white shorts and tennis shoes, a cap on his head and a racket gripped in his hands. I laughed the idea off. It was silly. I didn't know any of Ed's family. I hadn't really even known Ed, other than the few times we'd chatted at the courts. All I really knew was that Ed and his son loved tennis. That was as much of the story as I had ever gotten. So, no, I wouldn't try to fly to the funeral. It wouldn't be right.

So I did the next best thing. I got up from my desk, went down to the basement, and dug around until I found my old Prince tennis racket, the one with the oversized head. I hadn't played tennis more than once or twice in the last five years. I wiped off the racket and used some duct tape to cover a bare patch on the handle. After that, the racket was almost as good as new. Then I found an unopened can of balls, but when I pulled off the lid, there was no reassuring pop; the can must have gone flat. The balls wouldn't be any good for playing a match. But they were good enough for me.

I went back upstairs, put on my own white shorts and cap, and walked out the front door to find a tennis court.

Ed's son Danny had died in Vietnam. Now Ed was gone too. But Ed was wrong about the stories. Stories do last, Ed. You gave your story to me. And now I'm passing it on, like a crisp backhand swatting a fast serve back over the net.

Story Times

The first time
I saw you,
you were standing in a bus stop,
talking to a friend and laughing
in a high Irish voice.
It was cold that day,
and we had gotten
seventeen inches of snow,
a record,
but from where I stood,
I could see you smiling
like it was June.

The second time
you got into my car,
you started talking to me
about your day
as if this were already
the rest of our lives.
We were teaching, then,
and we used to sit around
telling jokes and stories,
helping students,
answering questions
about writing and math
and life.

Today
you are asleep,
and I am writing this
while the sun comes up
and the air is still filled with crickets.
It's fall now,
and in the afternoon
we'll go to a football game
and then have pizza with our friends,
and you'll be telling them stories
and smiling at me
from across the table.

Narrative Ideology

T he wind blows bitterly cold in Wisconsin during the winter months. One February, I fought the wind on my way to meet an old friend at the 602 Club. Even in my down-lined Green Bay Packers jacket, I was freezing. But that chill was an easy one compared with what was coming.

I was meeting an old friend I had bumped into a week earlier in a bookstore—Tasha. We'd gone to high school together, but I hadn't seen her since going to college. She told me she had just recently moved to Madison, where I had gone to school.

Small-town connections don't fade, and so it didn't take us long to be back talking a mile a minute. We sat drinking beers and recalling our past—teachers, friends, dances, sports, people we hated or missed. We told stories worth keeping.

I got her to laugh, retelling the great story of Mike and the turban.

Tasha kept laughing at the stories, but her laughter had an edge to it, not forced, but pushed out.

Eventually we couldn't put it off anymore, and we fell to talking about her marriage, how things had gone bad, and why she was getting a divorce.

"I've never been a quitter," she said. "Never had to give up, not on something important like this."

Looking at Tasha was like looking at patches of rainwater, dark, glistening, fading.

We talked on for a while. Tasha telling of some angry moment, a shouted exchange of bitter words.

"How the hell could he say that?" she said indignantly, pounding her fist onto the table and spilling a glass of Killian's Red across the table and onto me.

We both burst out laughing. "I see your point," I said, picking the glass back up and shaking one wet sleeve.

Literature's Separation from Life

That same winter I was also enrolled in an English class on picaresque novels. One of the books for that class was John Updike's *Rabbit, Run* (1960). It's about Harry "Rabbit" Angstrom, an unhappy man who leaves his wife in a desperate attempt to find himself and, perhaps, God. I was writing a paper about how Updike employed picaresque conventions to develop a theme of natural impulse versus genteel restraint. One convention I discussed was satire:

> [I]n standard picaresque fashion the whole novel satirizes marriage. Harry flees his marriage because he can't stand the commitment, but then within two days he is pretending to be married to Ruth when he makes love to her. Harry seems to have a psychological need for a mate. As Eccles describes it, "he's by nature a domestic creature" (146). Eccles himself believes marriage is sacred, and so he tries to reunite Harry and Janice. Strangely though, while working so hard to save the Angstroms' marriage, he allows his own marriage to go unattended to the point that his wife begins to consider adultery. And even Janice, who values her marriage so much that she drinks into oblivion rather than accept its collapse, finds that she sleeps better alone.
>
> Both Eccles and Janice claim to believe in the need for the social restraints of marital fidelity. Harry, on the other hand, supposedly believes in the need to follow one's impulses and flee those constraints. However, since all three characters' actions contradict their beliefs, Updike is able to satirize both the restriction and impulse sides of his conflict. Neither option seems to represent a good choice.

Looking at these two paragraphs again now, I can see how neatly they illustrate my theme. They use three different characters to prove that the impulse versus restraint conflict exists, yet show, at the same time, how Updike refuses to give the conflict a simple resolution. Thus the paragraphs help connect *Rabbit, Run* to the world of traditional literary criticism.

What the paragraphs don't do is connect *Rabbit, Run* to my own personal world. I had just learned that my friend Tahsa's marriage was falling apart, but my paper discussing a book that deals with the very same subject made no links between the two. I could have written how my friend's story was like Harry's. I could have examined how my own views of marriage and religion were evolving as a result of hearing these two stories. I could even have juxtaposed the story of my parents' twenty-five-year marriage with the stories of Harry's and my friend's marriages.

I didn't write any of these stories, though, because I was doing a conventional literary critique. I had a carefully chosen theme that I was trying to thoroughly analyze and discuss. I meticulously supported my analysis with quotes from the novel and citations of related works. I had taken a number of courses in my major that showed me what types of papers were well received, had already written a successful paper for this professor, and had even checked out a dozen books from the university library on Updike's novel to acquaint myself with the scholarly discourse on the subject. Unfortunately, not one of these reference points gave me an example of a connection to a personal, real-world story. Instead, everything centered on the world of Harry Angstrom, the world of books, the world of literature.

Telling Stories That Matter

But what about my own world? I like to believe that I read books to help me understand my own world better. Francis Spufford, a self-proclaimed fiction addict who traces some of reading's values in *The Child That Books Built*, says we have long valued books as tools that can help us grow:

> Once books were sacred, literally: the regime of reading was set by the experience of reading scripture. But in the secular times of the last three centuries . . . the promise of revelation has splintered, and the splinters have fallen separately, without losing all of their original brightness. One smithereen (at least) has glimmered in the novel. With its conventions that mimic the three dimensions of the world off the page, and its simulation of time passing as measured by experience's ordinary clocks, we hope it can bring a fully uttered clarity to the living we do, which is, we know, so hard to disentangle and articulate. And when it does, when a fiction does trip a profound recognition . . . the reward is more than an inert item of knowledge. The book becomes a part of the history of our self-understanding. The stories that mean most to us join the process by which we come to be securely our own. Literacy allows access to a huge force for development. (2002, 8–9)

Spufford is saying, in effect, that we value books, even works of fiction, for what they can teach us. Books give us knowledge of how to act in the world, how to live. It's a common view, something we may have picked up from industrious elementary reading teachers who were teaching us our ABCs.

Of course, like most everyone, I've also read just for fun. But as I have grown older and found the world to be more and more complex, I've become drawn to stories that help me make a little sense of what is often a very confusing existence. It's these slices of life that keep bringing me back to the libraries and the bookstores, always searching for another shred of understanding. This is also what led me to become an English literature major as an undergraduate, so that I could not only spend time reading about alternate experiences, but also have the chance to write about and discuss these new ideas.

Yet in my four years of pursuing a literature degree, I was never asked to write about the connections between the literary world and my own personal world. I don't know that anyone would have stopped me from doing that type of personal reflection—it just never occurred to me, any of my classmates, or, I think, any of my teachers. That wasn't how we understood the work of literary criticism. We were used to picking novels apart, dissecting them and scrutinizing each piece. We didn't explicitly try to add to our knowledge of a novel by linking it to our store of life experiences, at least not for our course papers.

I had learned this particular lesson so well that it took me several years to see how my friend's life might share a connection to Harry Angstrom's. That's what amazes me now. Not that I could have been taught literature by, say, Louise Rosenblatt's reader-response methods (Clifford 1991). There are always other teaching methods people could have employed. Perhaps some of them would have been more effective. But like so many students, I was happy with my education, liked most of my teachers, and wouldn't have wanted to change too much if you had asked me. Second-guessing doesn't interest me. What interests me is that I never saw the connection between the fictional world and my real world. It's easy to see now, but I couldn't see it then, not as I sat talking to Tasha.

The Narrative Instinct

Tasha needed help. She was hurting. No book had the answers, of course, and neither did I. But we knew we needed to share stories. A number of scholars have traced this human need to share stories. Critic and freelance author Kathryn Morton sees us as storytelling animals; she says, "Nothing passes but the mind grabs it and looks for a way to fit it into a story" (1986, 3). In fact, she says we can tell a baby is a human and not a pet when it begins demanding stories that connect the parts of its world (3).

Neil Postman, too, cites this need children have for stories that explain their connection to the real world:

> A story provides a structure for our perceptions; only through stories do facts assume any meaning whatsoever. This is why children everywhere ask, as soon as they have the command of language to do so, "Where did I come from?" and, shortly after, "What will happen when I die?" They require a story to give meaning to their existence. (1989, 122)

But we don't need researchers or theorists to tell us that stories are essential. We already know we need stories. We can't live without them. Every day we tell stories. They fill our conversations. We listen to them on the radio, read them in the newspaper, and watch them on T.V.

Our use of storytelling is even more profuse when we are young. Children spend most of their days inventing and then acting out all sorts of stories. Vivian Paley (1986) observes these storytelling activities in her kindergarten classroom:

> Social action in kindergarten is contained in dramatic plots. Since the characters create the plot, actors must identify themselves. In the doll corner, if a plumber arrives, then a pipe has just broken; the appearance of a schoolteacher signals that the children are about to receive a lesson. (1)

Paley says this storytelling helps kids learn their roles in society and how to interact with each other. While the children's story play does sometimes lead to stereotyped roles, it also allows for experimentation and exploration: "Every year, the girls begin with stories of good little families, while the boys bring us a litany of superheroes and bad guys. This kind of storytelling is an adjunct of play; it follows existing play and introduces new ideas for the future" (3). Our use of stories from such an early age shows that the drive to narrate experience is, if not instinctive, then at the very least quintessentially human.

Why Stories Were Banished from School

So we start out loving stories, and we continue to use them throughout our lives. Unfortunately, though, for every teacher like Paley who delights in hearing students tell stories, there are many more teachers who ask their pupils to push stories to the side in favor of "academic" learning. The process of banishing builds slowly and steadily throughout our educational experience.

Shirley Brice Heath, in her seminal ethnography, *Ways with Words* (1983), examines some of the early pressures on students to tell only certain kinds of stories in school, stories that often do not match the types of stories which children hear told in their homes and community settings. And this difference is often heightened along class and racial boundaries:

> For Roadville children, their community's ways of learning and talking about what one knows both parallel and contradict the school's approach to stories. . . . For Trackton children entering school, the problems presented by the school's conventions and expectations for story-telling are somewhat different. . . . The request [by a teacher] for a story which simply recounts facts accurately has no parallel in their community. (296)

The students in Heath's study must learn to perform stories for their teachers in often alien ways. Depending on their backgrounds, students are likely to have a range of difficulties figuring out the rules of school-based storytelling. They may, for example, have trouble deciding on the moral of a story, they may struggle with categorizations of fictive versus nonfictive, and they may not understand a teacher's request to summarize or introduce a story in a particular way.

In effect, one can argue that the teachers in Heath's study are asking students to move toward more abstract ways of handling stories, classifying and standardizing them. And before long, students learn that this is what teachers want; teachers prefer abstract learning, objective reasoning, distanced reflection. After a time, it becomes clear that even objectively looking at stories is not enough. As they mature and spend more time in the educational system, students eventually learn the central message that stories are not valued in school. Harold Rosen (1984) says schools force students to leave stories behind, that they strip students of their "story-telling rights," the very thing that gives meaning to language education:

> Childhood toys are superseded and put away or we hand them over to the younger ones. We are told that something called expository prose . . . is nothing less than the greatest intellectual achievement of Western civilization. It is in a state of achieved perfection called the Essay. . . . It is cleansed of ideology, purged of concreteness and the encumbrance of context. It soars into the high intellectual realm because, so it is said, it is "decontextualised." (26)

Joseph Trimmer explores similar biases against the educational use of stories in the introduction to his book *Narration as Knowledge* (1997). Courtney Cazden and Dell Hymes (1978) also argue that narrative communication is denigrated in education. And Walter Ong (2001) goes so far as to say that the very goals of literacy and the advancement of the human race are tied to our ability to use writing for abstraction and separation rather than narration.

Ong links stories to oral cultures and abstraction to literate cultures: "Primary oral culture also keeps its thinking close to the human life-world, personalizing things and issues, and storing knowledge in stories" (20). Ong claims that our ability to advance technically was linked to the power literacy gives us over time and space, that to advance we needed to move beyond what he implies was the primitive nature of oral communication, a type of communication rooted in narration. Ong says literacy prizes abstract reasoning: "Oral speech and thought narrativizes experience and the environment, whereas philosophy, which comes into being slowly after writing, is radically anti-narrative" (29). For Ong, literacy's ability to free humans from their context, to separate the knower from the known, is what raises human consciousness.

The effect of such biases against narrative is that, over time, stories are removed from any prominent role in our curriculum. We can see this in the common practice to start introductory composition courses by having students write a personal essay and then move on to the more "difficult" and "important" research paper. Narratives are viewed as an easy place to start, whereas the abstract essay is what is prized. Flower (1979) links narratives to writer-based prose and argues that students need to be taught how to move to the more academically suitable reader-based prose of the argumentative essay. And in trying to explain the difficulties basic writers have in learning to write at the collegiate level, David Bartholomae (1985) also illuminates the academy's antinarrative bias. In examining the conclusion to a basic writer's entrance examination essay, Bartholomae characterizes the writer's "problems" as follows:

> We get neither a technical discussion nor an *"academic" discussion* but a Lesson on Life [a narrative!]. This is the language [the basic writer] uses to address the general question, "How could two repairmen miss a leak?" The other brand of conclusion, *the more academic one,* would have required him to speak of his experience in *our terms*; it would, that is, have required a special vocabulary, a special system of presentation, and an interpretive scheme.... (137, emphasis added)

Bartholomae shows that academia is biased in favor of the abstract essay and against the narrative, adding that what students need to learn is how to write in the same muddy and confusing prose that scholars use. The clarity, the delight, the pleasure, and the meaning making that can all be found in stories, these are to be left to children. Too many people have worked to banish stories from our schools. And that has left us all out in a cold worse than any Wisconsin winter.

Awakening to Narrative

Despite its bias against narrative, our academic training doesn't prevent us from telling stories, of course. Tasha and I had no trouble trading tales from our high school days. What we missed at the time, though, at least in a conscious way, was how important these stories were to our health. Jeanne Smith (1994), in "The Story's the Thing," points out, "Telling stories makes me happy. There is something therapeutic for me in the process of selecting, developing, and telling a story" (8). Leslie Marmon Silko also discusses the power of stories for healing. In her novel *Ceremony* (1977), one of her characters claims that stories are much more than a form of amusement, stories are the only protection against sickness and death (2). Had you asked Tasha and me why we were using stories, though, it's doubtful we would have understood the health benefits of our story exchange. Instead, we most likely would have said we were just talking, not trying to use our stories to accomplish anything. That's why I think I missed linking Harry Angstrom's story to Tasha's at the time. I wasn't actively searching for stories to help Tasha with her marital problems. I didn't know one might do such a thing, that stories could be helpful in that way. Telling stories of younger days did make us feel better. But we wouldn't have attributed this to any special power of storytelling. We were just having a good time.

What I want to argue for now, though, is a conscious awakening to the narrative life. Certainly, I might have found a way to talk to Tasha about her troubles by sharing the story of *Rabbit, Run*. I might also have written about that book in a more personally valuable way had I used it as a means to reflect on my friend Tasha's problems. I wouldn't have expected a solution to these problems from telling and writing such stories. But a heightened awareness of the power of narrative would have promoted deeper understanding of the issues involved as well as greater opportunities to talk about those issues.

Narrative Ideology

I want to argue that narrative is more than a literary mode, a research method, a theory, or a teaching tool. Narrative is a way of life. Narrative is a set of beliefs. Narrative is an ideology.

I argued in Part One that it is perilous to adopt narrative approaches for teaching and research. People tend to look down on stories, to belittle them, to think they are just for children. There is, I have been trying to show, an antinarrative bias in academia.

Because there is some risk in pursuing narrative in one's work, I would argue that choosing to do so represents an ideological decision. In fact, it is the act of moving narratives to the core of your belief system that moves one into a narrative life.

In *Educational Development*, Kieran Egan (1979) offers us one definition of *ideology*, pulling it from a philosophical understanding of the term. Egan says, "The philosophic craving for generality is the means whereby chaotic particular knowledge about the world is reduced to manageable proportions" (53). In a sense, we have to develop some sort of structure to organize all the random stories of our lives. Recall Paley's discussion of the children's play stories. Children use stories of good families or heroes to develop notions of good and bad and how they will conduct themselves. A good person has to behave in a particular way. Such storytelling can help a person find a centralizing narrative for life.

Egan says that students learn to take general concepts, such as the concept of society or culture, and use them to form general principles for how the world operates:

> From these concepts and principles, [the students] form ideologies and metaphysical schemes; intellectual tools with which they can organize, simplify, and reduce even the greatest complexities with casual confidence. Ideologies and metaphysical schemes represent the boldest lines that give order to the students' mental map of the world. (54)

Egan says students use these ideologies to give meaning to the multiple details of life. Egan goes on to argue that while this generalizing weakens the storied nature of philosophic thinking, "there does remain, I think, a significant feature of the story form" (60–61).

The Russian scholar Volosinov (1973), considered by some a pen name for Bakhtin (Matejka and Titunik 1973, ix), links ideology directly to language. He claims that ideology does not depend on psychological understanding, but rather that psychology can be understood only via a study of ideology (13). It may not be too great an extrapolation to argue that if ideology is language-based, that language can be constituted in story form. Volosinov says, "Everything ideological possesses *meaning*: it represents, depicts, or stands for something lying outside itself. In other words, it is a *sign. Without signs, there is no ideology*" (9, emphasis in the original).

Volosinov illustrates how people add ideological value to physical objects, such as when a Christian uses bread and wine for the religious sacrament of communion. The bread and wine are only physical objects, but the ceremony imbues the objects with ideological meaning. For Volosinov, "a sign does not simply exist as a part of reality—it reflects and refracts another reality. Therefore, it may distort that reality or be true to it, or may perceive it from a special point of view, and so forth. . . . Wherever a sign is present, ideology is present, too" (10). If we consider the Christian sacrament again, we can see how it is the use of story that actually imbues the signs of bread and wine with ideological significance. In the story, Jesus Christ breaks bread and shares wine with his disciples the night before his Crucifixion. My interest is not in debating the truth of this story, but rather in showing that by retelling this story over and over, Christians imbue bread and wine with an ideological importance. It is sharing the story that is necessary to make sharing bread and wine at a Mass a sign, an ideological image.

In exploring the concept of ideology, I wish merely to argue that one's ideology can be focused on a narrative understanding of the world, that one can make the telling and hearing of stories a central part of one's agenda, a central goal that drives one to act in particular ways.

Terry Eagleton (1991) discusses the manner in which successful systems of ideology can actually cause people to begin to view beliefs as natural, as real and not ideologically driven. Eagleton says this process "involves ideology creating as tight a fit as possible between itself and social reality, thereby closing the gap into which leverage of critique can be inserted. When this happens, social reality is redefined by the ideology to become coextensive with itself" (58). Eagleton worries about the dangers of such uses of ideology. This can cause people to accept one group's beliefs as natural laws that can't be redefined.

Eagleton is right to fear the misuse of ideology, because one does not have to look very far to find examples of belief systems being turned into norms. Consider again my discussion of the antinarrative bias in education. The idea that an argumentative essay exhibits the pinnacle of intellectual thought is a belief, not a fact. Yet for years the writing of essays has been treated by English teachers as a much more important goal than the writing of narratives. Teaching students the ability to write a good essay is perhaps the single most common goal of composition courses across the United States and probably the world. While teachers would also like their students to be able to write well in multiple genres, including the writing of strong narratives, it is essay writing that most composition teachers focus their efforts upon. Teachers do this because essays are viewed as the most important form of writing, as the central mode of academic discourse. The well-written essay has become a sign of intellectual growth and achievement. And this is where we see that the essay has become an ideological tool. The essay has intellectual and academic value only because we have assigned those values to it. We could, instead, have assigned those values to the well-written narrative. But we didn't. And that is one reason why first-year composition is the most widely required course in United States universities, but it is separated from creative writing, an elective course in which students are asked to write stories.

Given the pervasiveness of antinarrative views, then, choosing to adopt a narrative ideology engages one in a struggle with the status quo, puts one at odds with one's department, one's university, even society. At the same time, however, enacting a narrative ideology does not have to take place on such a grand scale. Often, following a narrative ideology merely affects the decisions an individual makes.

Let me offer, then, a simple example of how adopting a narrative ideology might influence the choices one teacher makes. At my university, like many, we require students to take an introductory literature course. There are many different ways to teach this course, from a literary analysis approach to a reader-response approach. Fortunately, my university offers teachers freedom to design the course as they see fit. Any literature course involves the reading of stories. So that in itself does not represent a full participation in the narrative life. As I've said, we all tell stories all the time.

What separates the casual user of stories from the narrative ideologue can be seen in how one might teach this literature course. The narrative way to teach this course would be to make the act of storytelling the driving force of the course. Once promoting narrative thinking becomes one's goal, the course's design becomes focused on having students tell and respond to stories. So, the course might be structured to start with fairy tales, fables, and legends, some of the stories students would have been exposed to as children. A narrative teacher doesn't want to simply examine stories in a detached way. That's too much like dissection. So rather than simply critique, analyze, and pull apart these fairy tales, a narrative teacher would ask students to respond to the fairy tales they were reading by writing fairy tales of their own.

What a narrative teacher tries to do is engage students with the excitement and power of storytelling. From fairy tales, students could move to reading other types of stories, even those we might call "serious" fiction or classic works of the canon, such as the works of Raymond Carver (1982) or Ernest Hemingway (1966). But again, the narrative teacher would not spend tedious hours asking students to study themes and symbolism and foreshadowing. At least, the teacher wouldn't ask students to study these solely from analysis of the stories being read. Instead, students would move from reading stories to writing their own "serious" fiction.

And a narrative teacher would be open to all sorts of stories, romantic novels, comic books, and sports stories. All stories are useful. Students might also tell the stories of their own literacy lives as a part of this course, tracing their reading and writing experiences over a lifetime. Perhaps students would even be asked to begin writing their own novels. Imagine that.

In essence, the narrative teacher believes in the power of stories, and so stories become a central tool for teaching and learning. Living the narrative life means rethinking one's whole approach to knowledge. Rather than always pursuing knowledge through analysis and critical thinking that rely on critiquing and dissecting ideas, narrative believers seek to create knowledge through the telling of stories. Storytelling becomes a goal in this system, not an afterthought or a nice diversion. In another work, *Teaching as Story Telling*, Kieran Egan (1986), whom I discussed earlier in terms of his theorizing about ideology, explores how our entire educational system would be different if it were built around an active use of narrative theory. Egan, I think, is living the narrative life. His ideology is narrative in nature.

Central Tenets of Narrative Ideology

There are a number of tenets that make up narrative ideology. These ideas seem to be common ground for people interested in pursuing a narrative approach to life. Of course, ideologies are far too complex to unpack completely. But what I wish to do here is discuss some of the key beliefs that are central to a narrative view of the world.

Meaning Comes Through Stories

Most central, I believe, to the development of a narrative ideology is adopting a belief in the meaning-making power of stories. With Dawn Abt-Perkins, I have looked at the ways young science students sometimes turn to stories to make sense of research findings when more objective scientific explanations fail them:

> I couldn't seem to make sense of it. We did this experiment in exercise physiology, and I thought I would write about that, but I couldn't. . . . But when I made up this story, I seemed to understand everything better. . . . Brandon's story provided a context in which the experiment became meaningful. (Pagnucci and Abt-Perkins 1992, 54–55)

At the core of narrative ideology is this way of seeing the world through stories. Yes, there are plenty of other ways to interpret events, but events make sense for some people, like this young scientist, only when they are cast in the form of a story. I recall once my doctoral advisor, David Schaafsma, telling me about a job interview at which he was questioned on his use of narrative research techniques. "How can you prepare our students to do research without giving them a background in statistics?" someone asked.

"I don't believe in statistics," Schaafsma said. From a narrative perspective, isolated facts and numbers are not enough to explain the world. Instead, we wish for thick stories that capture events in their full detail.

Resisting Closure

In narrative ideology, there are always other possibilities for understanding events. Narratives always leave open the door for reinterpretations. Harold Rosen (1986) says that "a basic form of narrative is not only telling but also *re*telling and this includes our willingness to hear some stories retold" (230, emphasis in the original). Since retelling is a natural part of the storytelling process, there is always a chance that any given story will be recast, reinterpreted. This means stories never offer fixed answers, definitive accounts. Someone can always say, "But what if . . . ," or "Perhaps this . . . ," or "It could have gone like this. . . . " Rosen says narratives are nothing more than a scrutiny of "a never-ceasing, unstoppable infinity of events without beginning or end" (230). We use narratives to make some sort of interpretation of the world as it passes us, but this interpretation is always just one of many. As Rosen points out, "To begin a story is to make a choice from an infinity of possibilities, selecting one set rather than another" (231).

David James Duncan (1995) offers similar insight in explaining his concept of "river teeth," "hard, cross-grained whorls of memory that remain inexplicably lodged in us. . . . These are our 'river teeth'—the time-defying knots of experience that remain in us after most of our autobiographies are gone" (4). While Duncan says river teeth are sometimes mere shells of former stories, they are still a part of our narrative, grappling with existence: "eternity itself possesses no beginning, middle or end. Fossils, arrowheads, castle ruins, empty crosses . . . what moves us about many objects is not what remains but what has vanished" (5). Duncan's notion of river teeth calls to mind those essential stories that stick with us over the years, the ones we never totally let go of. Yet, at the same time, Duncan makes us aware of the fleeting power of memory. He says we have "to let go of what can't be saved, to honor what can and perhaps to make others more aware of, and more willing to accept and share, the same cycle in themselves" (5). Perhaps we can never lay claim to any one story since all stories slip through our grasp over the years. We can hang on, but the river of time keeps passing us by.

Rather than offer a definitive answer, a closed reading, Richard Meyer (1996) suggests that we frame stories to provide our view of them: "Any story we tell or write is framed in some way. A frame is a point of view, perspective, stance, or relationship that is a foundational part of a story" (119). In discussing framing, Meyer says stories call in the voices of other people, other writers. Sometimes these other voices fit the frames we've built for our stories, sometimes they run contrary to them (130). Meyer helps us understand that every story is told from a particular viewpoint, but it can always be retold from another perspective. No one frame is the definitive answer for any given story. Each frame is just one more lens of understanding, and the lenses can always be changed. There is no closure in the narrative life, only moments of clarity.

The Centrality of Art

When you live the narrative life, you are not content with dry, dull academic prose. Narrative ideology sees the world as filled with lively stories. If this is the case, why should we accept flat, lifeless prose? How many jargon-heavy, obfuscating, theoretically overbearing journal articles have been published in the academy? Hundreds of thousands, I'm sure. Yet how many have been read, understood, and put into practice? How many of these articles have made any difference at all?

Now certainly writers are all free to choose their own style. That's one of the beauties of the written word, its endless variety. And yet, why have journal editors so rarely chosen to include educational narratives among their offerings? Why has the style of academese been developed into a form of lifeless, brittle prose, mostly devoid of even those simplest of words that best connect us to writing: *you* and *I?*

In adopting a narrative ideology, one comes to believe that writing ought to be about art. That a research report ought to help us live in someone else's shoes, not simply hear what kind of shoes the person was wearing. Throughout this book, then, I've woven a range of stories and anecdotes to help connect you, through stories, to my arguments.

As much as we strive for accuracy in academic work, we ought, as well, to be striving for language that shakes our world up, rearranges it, and makes us pause and look again. Murray (2002) says we need to choose words that offer "surprise or tension or interaction that comes from the collision of the words" (8). Or, as he puts it more artfully, "I hear myself say, for no reason I understand, 'the melancholy of a sunny day,' and hear something that is akin to music" (8). Murray is pushing us to write as if we were making music, not just academic arguments. I admit, that's a tall order. But the art of a story is what is valued within a narrative ideology. The poet Gianfranco Pagnucci says, in the poem "A Red Fox Again," "I see all our lives together strung in small bright beads of light" (1991, 29). This is narrative ideology, seeing the world's stories as moments of art, beads of light.

The Fluidity of Truth

In a narrative world, there is no such thing as a fixed truth. Stories are always fluid, moving, changing. To narrative ideology, the world is Bakhtin's concept of "heteroglossia," which Bakhtinian scholar Michael Holquist (1990) explains as "a way of conceiving the world as made up of a roiling mass of languages, each of which has its own distinct formal marker. These features are never *purely* formal, for each has associated with it a set of distinctive values and presuppositions" (69, emphasis in the original). Languages for Bakhtin are a product of the social, historical, and cultural forces that have affected the speakers of those languages. Every utterance is unique, and language is remade with each utterance spoken or written. In such a world, the notion of any sort of fixed truth quickly dissipates, carried away in the swirl of the waters of heteroglossia. There cannot be any fixed truth because the words to describe it are always being modified over time by individuals. We can't, for example, even agree on exactly what a simple word like *chair* means. To one person, the word *chair* means a wooden object that sits in a kitchen to be used as a person eats. But to another person, the word *chair* can mean the throne where a tyrant sits. Every word is viewed from a different perspective depending on who is using the word.

In terms of stories, we already know how fluid truth is. Get together with family members and it's easy to hear many different accounts of the same incident, all dependent upon who is telling the story. Ask a question like, "Who broke this lamp?" and what's true for me will be completely untrue for my brother. Certainly, there are facts in the world, simple facts like broken lamps and more horrific facts like the perpetration of the Holocaust. But the interpretation of facts through stories is always changing. We can agree that there are facts, but we can never agree on exactly the same interpretation of those facts. Probably the best we can do is to get twelve jurors to agree, and even then, such agreement is rare.

But is the lack of a fixed truth such a bad thing? I think, actually, that stories can help us get at the truth even if there isn't a firm truth to be had. In a short story about the Vietnam War called "How to Tell a True War Story," Tim O'Brien (1990a) tries to break us out of our fixation on the truth. He wants us to see that the idea of Truth with a capital *T* actually limits our ability to understand the world. Hence he makes the claim, "in a true war story nothing is ever absolutely true" (88). We might wonder how this can be. Yet O'Brien says what actually happened isn't nearly as important as our memory of what happened. We reconstruct the truth in our minds until our story of what happened is truer than what *really* happened. O'Brien says it is extremely difficult to separate what happens from what seems to happen (78). What interests O'Brien, then, is getting at the truth of our emotional experience. "Absolute occurrence is irrelevant. A thing may happen and be a total lie; another thing may not happen and be truer than the truth" (89).

O'Brien knows that the past is slippery and that our minds are forgetful. What's more, we know from Bakhtin that we will see accounts of the world from radically different positions anyway. We can never understand a war story or any story the same as anyone else. Our past always reconstructs the events for us. Maybe we have a friend who died in a war or an uncle who led a student demonstration against it. Maybe we've learned one story, but the real story has never been told. Or we've tried to tell a particular story, but no matter how much we revise, we just can't get it to come out right. Language often fails us, especially when the emotional stakes are high. O'Brien says he writes stories trying to save himself from the horror of his experiences in the war. But for all the truth he may or may not tell in his stories, he's not trying to forget the war. What he wants to do is remember the war in a way that lets him understand it. There are no truths in a narrative life, only different ways to tell the story.

The Pleasure of Messiness

One of the beauties of narratives is that they don't wrap things up in neat packages. Narratives can address contradiction, confusion, and complexity without offering any concrete answers, which is, upon consideration, exactly what real life does. We struggle in life to deal with conflicting emotions, misguided agendas, and mistaken analyses. Stories can capture the unsettled nature of living, the messiness of existence. In a story, nothing is ever quite perfect.

Kathy Carter (1993) believes it is the ability of narrative to capture complexity that makes it such a powerful form of knowledge:

> At one level, story is a mode of knowing that captures in a special fashion the richness and the nuances of meaning in human affairs. We come to understand sorrow or love or joy or indecision in particularly rich ways through the characters and incidents we become familiar with in novels or plays. This richness and nuance cannot be expressed in definitions, statements of fact, or abstract propositions. It can only be demonstrated or evoked through story. (6)

Accepting messiness is a useful characteristic for an ideology. This makes narrative ideology a flexible system of belief. Any number of stories, even stories in diametric opposition, can exist within a narrative view of the world.

David Schaafsma (1993) sees narrative as a valuable research reporting tool for exactly this reason: "I am celebrating, I hope, the varied voices of teachers—and some students—because their voices in my story help preserve some sense of the complexity of their lives, and the complexity of their experiences with literacy learning in the inner city" (xviii). In *Eating on the Street*, Schaafsma tries to capture this sense of complexity by examining an educational conflict through the voices of six different teachers. As each teacher reinterprets from his or her perspective a moment of crisis, a culture-based conflict over whether black children should be allowed to eat on the street, we come to see conflicting views and overlapping agreements, dissension and unity. Through multiple stories, we come to better understand the broad ramifications of one moment in time.

Multiple stories can also save us from being forced to toss aside outlying data that does not fit the current theoretical perspective; a storied view can adjust to encompass the new, unusual data set. Of course, this means that when one seeks understanding through narrative means, the conclusions drawn may not measure up to the exacting demands of the scientific method. That is as it should be. It's important to remember that narrative ideology is only one set of beliefs and that there is room for other sets. Where narrative may fail in its exactitude, it offers instead a way to deal with overwhelming complexity, to handle a cacophony of thoughts and ideas. Ideologies are most useful when they are adopted consciously. Thus when one chooses complexity, this has to be done with the knowledge that some of the exact measures may be lost. Though stories can preserve details in all their clarity, the narrative form also allows for continual reinterpretation of those details. Living the narrative life means learning to take pleasure in unruly answers.

Milan Kundera (1988) also discusses the value of confusion in his work *The Art of the Novel*: "Irrational logic is based on the mechanism of confusion: Pasenow [one of the protagonists in Kundera's *Sleepwalkers* trilogy] has a poor sense of reality; the causes of events escape him . . . yet although it may be disguised, unrecognizable, causeless, the external world is not mute: it speaks to him. . . . One thing is like another, is confounded with it . . . and thus through its likeness makes itself clear" (60–61). For Kundera, understanding comes through juxtaposition, through confusion. This is the power of the novel, the narrative; to illuminate things that at first seem to be undecipherable. Narrative ideology is built on a trust in confusion, a letting go of certainty and clarity that can ultimately lead to understanding.

Retelling Academia

I've already discussed the fact that adopting a narrative ideology brings one into conflict with the status quo and more entrenched ideologies. So while my university allows people to teach introductory literature any way they see fit, I know my narrative-based approach is far from the norm. Studying literature via story writing flies in the face of many years of literary criticism, the bedrock on which most English departments are built. So the act of telling stories can rock foundations. But that's risky business. To choose the narrative life is to take some chances.

Unfortunately, once you discover the power of stories, there's no going back. The power of narrative ideology becomes self-evident. Eagleton warns us about this danger, but the problem is, when you first write down one of your own stories and find that it illuminates some belief of yours that was previously hidden, the power of your own narrative voice overwhelms you.

The notion of using writing for self-discovery is not a new one. Self-discovery has long been a driving motivation for writers. Consider these words from Annie Dillard (1989):

> When you write, you lay out a line of words. The line of words is a miner's pick, a woodcarver's gouge, a surgeon's probe. . . . The line of words is a hammer. You hammer against the walls of your house. You tap the walls, lightly, everywhere. After giving many years' attention to these things, you know what to listen for. Some of the walls are bearing walls; they have to stay, or everything will fall down. Other walls can go with impunity; you can hear the difference. Unfortunately, it is often a bearing wall that has to go. It cannot be helped. There is only one solution, which appalls you, but there it is. Knock it out. Duck. (3–4)

Dillard's explanation of the act of writing is all about discovery. And, in so many ways, she's correct. When we write, we make discoveries, particularly when we write the stories of our lives. Once you realize this, you don't want to give it up. It becomes a belief, an ideology: stories have the power to teach us.

Narrative ideology then, strives to challenge our educational establishment. Narrative ideology wants to reinvent school, to retell it, by placing stories at the center of our teaching and learning. Instead of research reports, narrative ideology wants us to tell stories. Instead of the writing of dissertation studies, narrative ideology seeks the writing of dissertation novels. The narrative life is an ideological one. It is a system of values. Adopting it means taking up the challenge of those who belittle and denigrate stories. While there are many ideologies to choose from, once a person chooses narrative ideology, that person is choosing to fight. But it's a long battle, one I fight one student and one class at a time. I tell a story here, listen to a story there, and ask a student to write a story over yonder. In discussing narrative as an ideological position, I have tried to draw out the many ramifications of this political stance. But, at the same time, such talk can be alarming, off-putting. Ultimately, narrative ideology is about coming to believe in the power of stories.

Living the Narrative Life

When we live the narrative life, we learn to trust more in stories. We choose them more consciously, share them more eagerly, and preserve them more carefully. Looking back now, I understand what really matters is that I have this story of Tasha at all. I've written it down, thought about it again and again, and now it has become one of the stories I treasure. I don't know what became of Tasha or even where she is today. Our friends come and go. But I have a small story of her—talking, smiling, laughing.

We ought to seek out stories. Even our troubles, the broken-down car, the lost treasure, the embarrassing fall: when we become attuned to the ways these events create a storied life, they lose some of their bite, becoming, with some time and distance, moments to treasure. Once, walking out of an Eric Clapton concert that had cost $85 per ticket, I heard a tall blonde man say to the friend next to him: "Sure, it was expensive, but what are your memories worth?"

Eric Clapton sitting on a bright stage, his eyes closed, quietly strumming "Tears in Heaven" (1992). Tasha's small hands twitching in the air, her voice edged and her eyes gleaming and my left sleeve damp from her spilled beer. And Updike's character Harry, Rabbit, in anguish over the loss of his baby, his marriage a shambles, searching for answers, for some sort of direction and purpose:

> Rabbit comes to the curb but instead of going to his right and around the block he steps down, with as big a feeling as if this little side street is a wide river, and crosses. He wants to travel to the next patch of snow. Although this block of brick three-stories is just like the one he left, something in it makes him happy; the steps and windowsills seem to twitch and shift in the corner of his eye, alive. This illusion trips him. His hands lift of their own and he feels the wind on his ears even before, his heels hitting heavily on the pavement at first but with an effortless gathering out of a kind of sweet panic growing lighter and quicker and quieter, he runs. (284)

Living the narrative life is about figuring out what counts. It's about becoming a seeker and teller of stories. The narrative life isn't for everyone. Stories can be too full of pain. Stories can bring life into too sharp a focus. Stories can hurt us. But, in the end, they're all we have. Stories are what we believe in. Narratives are what form our ideology.

It's risky to follow the narrative life, to cast aside the comforts and securities of tradition, to take a different path. But once stories grab you, once you see their power, there is no going back to sleep. You lift your hands, feel the wind rise, and take to your feet. Stories tell us where to go. That's what I realized. One day, the old world of academia, the world of objectivity and argument and distance and reason, it just wasn't enough anymore. I felt cut off from what mattered. I found I couldn't hear my friends, couldn't hear Tasha's sadness, couldn't hear the stories that mattered. They had been blocked from me. And so, like Harry, I started to run. I had to get away, escape the prison whose bars I had stumbled upon. Narrative ideology is like any other belief system: once you find it, you wonder how you ever existed before. One day, I woke up and realized that I needed to live a narrative life if I was going to have any kind of life at all.

Sharing Stories

It's a story about. . . .

> This is my story.
> Actually, that sounds a lot like my story.
> I know that story too.
> So who's story is it, then?

I like personal writing, but it needs to be fun. I don't want a lot of tragedy in there.

> **I experimented with that.**

It was fun.

> I wrote about my ugly thoughts about my students.

I also have this problem of keeping my mouth shut when I'm telling a story.

This story seems so simple.
> *I'm glad to know it's OK to tell a simple story.*

> Well . . . that *won't* be *the story* this time.

There aren't any good women left.
> I *know* what *that* story's about.
> Sorry, *I* have nothing to contribute to *that* conversation.

> **I can't make this frame work.**
> **These quotes feel *so* artificial somehow.**
> **These references just don't fit in my story.**

57

When I first got hired as a teacher, they said, could I be the librarian or the basketball coach?

I said, How about I'll be the storyteller?

They said they really needed a coach.

I *think* I figured it out. . . .

I had to make up things that could have been true, might've been true.

If you can't find it, make it up.

Where am I going with this?

What a fascinating *story.*

Of course, that's cause it's my *story.*

Teachers tell stories all the time.

It's so central to the way I teach that I don't even think about it.

I'm not cut out to be a teacher.

I love to teach.

He was an excellent teacher.

She was just scary.

He was *not* into being nurturing.

I wasn't called to be a teacher.

I got into teaching to teach.

I wish I could teach like that.

She taught by telling stories.

Why are we talking about stories again? Aren't we supposed to be eating lunch?

That's the story I *should* have written.

Is that *Wholly* or *Holy?*

You didn't get to read that part of the story.

Why are we attacking her story, when the racist's story was OK?

For *those* readers who *have* page numbers.

Oh yeah, I'm writing in third person, but, pleassseee . . . it's me.

I'd really like to read these stories.

I kept feeling dishonest.

Can't you be a little less pompous in your style?
The story went downhill from there....

Everything in my story is true
because I'm not *imaginative* and *creative*
and *I couldn't make the stuff up* . . .
well . . . I guess a few things are made up.

I'm kind of interrupting . . .
but *I've* already interrupted.

I've got a story about that.

I'm sort of like your teacher, the old school, crusty kind.
Versus the kind of teacher I really am or want to be.

This isn't really about your story, but . . .

It seemed like the right voice.
It seemed like the right story.

That moment.

Interesting how you can change an entire story by how you frame it.
Interesting how you can change the whole story with just a few words.
You could change the story by telling the truth.
You could make it better by lying.

Objective Truth.

Probably I should have written this story years ago.

I knew I could get into a whole lot of trouble with this story . . .
and yet I hardly hesitated.

This voice is more genuine.

I had never written a teacher narrative.

Where did the storytellers all go?

without stories we're lost

But are narratives really research?

Who's asking the question?

How can this be a true story ... if I just made it up?

Alright now, did I just make that up?
        I absolutely *don't* remember it that way.
                But now I think that's how it was.

The *yearbook* made an error.
        Books do make mistakes.
            Yeah, even history books do.

Kathy was an expert on pickles, by the way.
That was her story.
I liked it.
I thought it was weird.
That's why I liked it.

The story I was gonna tell *still* hasn't been told.

We need stories from teachers in the trenches.

If I move this *here*, what would be true then?

That's the sad thing about teachers,
they're dead by the time you appreciate the stories they told.

How do you get to the truth?

How does that story go again?

The Writing Project *insists* on narratives.
        Then the Grants Office sends it back and asks, where are the *numbers?*
           Administration will take that under advisement.

I've *never* written like *this* before.

He was the *most* annoying child in the universe.
    I *know* that kid.
        Yeah, and boy could he tell some stories.

Sticking to the *facts* becomes slippery.

I recognized the quote and, *what was more,* I think I *understood* it.

So to sum up, *none* of us knows where we're going.
That's OK. It'll be a better story that way.

At least when bad things happen to you,
they make for good stories.

There it is.

Who's telling the story?

And they lived happily ever after.
I'd like to live happily ever after.

And then what happened?

Read it again.

Just one more story.

PART THREE

The Baseball Card Collection

There were three of us sitting by the lake that day. It was early July, but cool for that time of year, and the breeze off the water seemed to add to the overcasting of the sky.

We were sitting on the terrace behind the student union. There was a pretty good crowd even with the gray sky, and as I leaned back in my chair I could see a steady stream of people going in and out of the building.

We were drinking Garten Brau Dark out of paper cups that left a taste of wax in your mouth along with the beer. Andrew and Dave were talking about the class they'd taught that morning. It was the last day of their summer program, the Wisconsin Writing Project. They'd been working with high school kids from all over the state, and their students had published a book, *Scribblers Anonymous*.

Things had come together for them, the way they often do.

"Then Latisha showed me this great poem she'd written, about her dad leaving," said Andrew.

"But she didn't want to put it into the book?" asked Dave.

"No. I asked her that. But she liked the story about her soccer team better."

"Safer, I suppose," said Dave.

"Yeah," said Andrew.

I watched a woman trying to balance on a bike while she talked to a couple friends. She had one hand stretched out to the wall to hold herself steady, but the bike was a little too high for her, and so she couldn't plant her feet firmly on the ground.

"So the program's all finished?" I asked.

"Yeah, today was the last day," said Andrew.

"How long was it?"

"Six weeks."

"Some of the other teachers are going to stop by," Dave said.

"What about you?" asked Andrew. "You had your defense today, right? Is it 'Doctor' Gian now?" he laughed.

"I suppose," I said. "Well, once the university recognizes it."

"How long does that take?"

"Who knows?" I said. "I guess after all the paperwork goes through."

"And you pay the last bill," said Dave.

"But you're done, now, right?" Andrew said.

"Basically. I've got some revisions to do, still, but it's just Dave and me now."

"Right," said Dave, and he lifted his glass toward me.

"Actually, things went pretty . . . "

"Hey guys." A man and two women were walking up to the table. One of the women sat down between Andrew and me. I thought I remembered that her name was Sharon. The other two people introduced themselves, but there was a lot of talking going on at the next table, and I couldn't catch the names.

Everybody started talking all at once—Andrew to Sharon, Dave to the other two new arrivals—so I just sat and drank my beer, looking around. The woman on her bike was gone. I watched a guy carry a bag of popcorn and three beers down the steps.

"So, do you teach here in Madison?" I asked Sharon.

"In Middleton, actually," she said.

"Oh, how do you like that?"

"It's a pretty good school," she said.

Some more people joined us. It was getting a little cold, and I wished I had brought a jacket.

"Didn't they try to get a new referendum for a school out there?" Andrew asked.

"Yes, they did. But it got voted down."

"That's too bad," I said.

"Yeah," said Sharon, "They approved money to extend the highway to the interstate, but they won't pay for a decent sized school. Next year's freshman class is supposed to be 300 students bigger than we can handle."

"Times are tough," I said. "The whole economy is in a downturn, they say."

"Hey," said Andrew. "I know what you could do to raise some money. Why don't you write to that the girl, what's her name, Tiffany or something like that?"

"Who?" said Sharon.

"You know," I interjected. "Tiffany Grey. She's the woman who married that 90-year-old millionaire. She's only about 25, I think."

"Oh, right," said Sharon. "I think I saw that on T.V."

"See?" said Andrew. "She's going to be rich soon. Maybe she'll give you some money to add a room to your school."

"Yeah, right," laughed Sharon.

"Oh, but she says she loves him," I said.

"Yeah, sure," said Andrew.

"It's really bad when that happens," said another woman.

"Sorry," I said, "I didn't catch your name."

"It's Jessica," she said.

"I'm Gian," I said, and extended my hand. "Don't you think the old guy knows exactly why she's marrying him?" I said. "He's got to."

"I'm not so sure," said Jessica. "This actually happened to my family. My uncle was eighty-seven when he married this woman in her twenties."

"Hunh," said Dave.

"So, what happened?" I asked.

"Well, she went after all his money."

"Right."

"But that wasn't the worst thing. I mean the family didn't really care much about the money. He had some, but not a whole lot. The thing was, she wouldn't let us have anything. None of the furniture or the heirlooms. She's just selling all that stuff off. Some things have been with the family for years. Like a clock my grandmother had."

"That's pretty bad," said Dave.

"The worst thing is, she won't give us any of the photographs. She won't let us have anything. But I mean what does she need all those photographs for? They're not of her family, even. I mean, the money's one thing, but why won't she give us the stuff that really matters?"

Jessica looked pretty upset about the whole thing.

"Sorry," she said. "It just makes me so mad."

"So what's your family going to do?" I asked.

"Well, it's all in court now, but the trouble is, she could throw out a lot of stuff in the meantime. Maybe she already has."

"What a world this is," I said.

"Yeah," said Dave. "People are a little crazy."

We all laughed a little and then Andrew said, "I have a story that's similar to that. Well, it's not really on a par with that at all, I guess, but you reminded me of the time my wife made me give away my baseball card collection."

We laughed at the comparison, and then Andrew began to tell his story.

"My wife and I were trying to clean out the basement. You know the way things pile up and every few years you try to go through it and make a little more order."

"Right," said somebody.

"Well, we had this friend who had a twelve-year-old son who really loved baseball, and my wife thought it would be a nice thing to give him my old baseball card collection. But, of course, I didn't want to. I mean, I had some good cards in there. Like Pete Rose in his prime, and Hank Aaron, and Reggie Jackson in his record year."

"Hey, those would be worth some money," said Dave.

"I know. Exactly," said Andrew. "Well anyway, my wife kept saying, 'you never look at any of them, and you're not going to sell them, so why not pass them on to somebody who can really appreciate them?' And I kept resisting this idea but finally, I thought, maybe she's right."

"So, we were over there one day having a cookout, and when we were about to leave, my wife kept saying, go on, tell him. Bobby. That's the kid's name. So I did, but even as I was handing him the box, I knew it was a mistake."

"Well the kid's face lights up and he tears through the box. The rest of us are standing around talking, and my wife is kidding me about the cards, and then Bobby runs off to his room, and comes back with one of those price books. 'Look at this,' he says. 'This one's worth fifteen dollars.' And he is grinning from ear to ear. And you know, I just wanted to smack that smug smile off his face, but what could I do?"

We all started to laugh again.

"You know, and I don't want to seem like I'm just whining or anything, but I could remember getting all those cards. And filing them in the box. I mean that was part of my growing up. But I suppose I'm dwelling on it too much."

"It's funny, Andrew. That's the second time I've heard you tell that story. So it must have really had an impact on you," I said.

"I mean, I know they're only baseball cards, but . . . ," Andrew trailed off.

"But it's the stories, in the cards, right?" said Jessica. "Like my uncle's stuff. You need that stuff, to help you remember the stories."

"Exactly," said Andrew.

"Like, I remember, I have, I mean, I had this one Johnny Bench card. It wasn't a rookie card or anything. But the thing was, when I was in first grade, this kid named Todd, he was really good at sports and stuff. Well, one day, he says to me, 'Andrew, Johnny Bench is the greatest baseball player ever.' And then he handed me that card. And I had kept it ever since. I *never* should have given away those cards," said Andrew.

"Water under the bridge," said Dave.

"Tell you what," I said to Andrew. "Next time I'm at Walgreen's, I'll buy you some baseball cards."

"Great," said Andrew. "I guess that's what I have to do, start over."

"Sure," said Jessica. "You could do that. But not us, we can't get back our stories."

Visions

It takes *perfect* balance
to cross the old tree trunk
above the foaming river.
Only you can cross it.

Then a *tough* climb along
a winding mountain trail.
In one spot, the path has crumbled away,
and you must jump across
a thousand foot drop.
Only you can make it.

Finally,
at the top of the mountain,
the path *almost* disappears
into the trees.
Only you can find it.

The path goes into a dark forest,
and leads to a *gnarled* tree.
You *dig* in the leaves
at the foot of the tree,
and find an ancient red rock.
As dusk falls,
the rock begins to glow.
And *only you* can see it.

—*Gian Pagnucci and Edel Reilly*

Telling Your Own Story

Maxwell Street Days

"You can each have a nickel to buy one comic book," said my mom to my brother, Rob, and me. It was Maxwell Street Day in Platteville, Wisconsin, the first Friday in August 1973. I had not yet entered the first grade.

In those days, Maxwell Street Day was a giant community garage sale. People from all over the county would line Main Street from top to bottom with tables of clothes, books, antiques, jewelry, fishing lures, and used tools. The regular stores on Main Street also put out tables with sale items, and there were hot dog stands and burgers and cotton candy. There were lots of good deals and lots of talking with friends and neighbors. But the best part was looking for treasure among all the junk.

I can't remember what Rob bought that day, but I bought a copy of *The Justice League of America* (Fox 1968). The cover was missing, but the splash page showed a cave of superheroes trapped in standing coffins that the villain, the nefarious T. O. Morrow, was striding past in triumph. Batman was one of the heroes in that issue, and I bought the comic because I somehow knew who he was, even though neither the live-action Batman television show nor the Super Friends animated cartoon had yet come to television in the Platteville area. Not that we would have been able to pick up either show at our house on Mockingbird Road. We lived seven miles from the town and could pick up only two television stations, both of them fuzzy.

Childhood's Storied Roots

The stories of our childhoods shape us forever. The eminent narrative scholar and children's teacher Vivian Paley says children are instinctive storytellers who learn to understand the world through the telling of these narratives:

> Amazingly, children are born knowing how to put every thought and feeling into story form. If they worry about being lost, they become the parents who search; if angry, they find a hot hippopotamus to impose his will on the world. Even happiness has its plot and characters: "Pretend I'm the baby and you only love me and you don't talk on the telephone." . . . Somewhere in each fantasy is a lesson that promises to lead me to questions and commentary, allowing me to glimpse the universal themes that bind together the individual urgencies. (1990, 4)

From the beginning, we are telling stories to figure out who we are and where our place is in the world. But my purpose here is not to prove this fact to you. You already know it to be true. All you need to do is pause for a moment and remember your childhood: what did you care about then, who were you, what stories can't you forget? Paley, as she explores this issue of the power of childhood stories, identifies one of her own central narratives: "Indeed, my strongest childhood memories are of the daily chase of good and bad guys on the playground. Was I part of it or did I only watch? Silently I replayed the dialogues during the school day, and a note I wrote to someone—or perhaps it was written to me—reappears in my mind even today. 'What will you be? Can we pretend sisters?'" (5). Hearing Paley's memory, it's easy to imagine a touch of longing in her voice: perhaps she was an only child; perhaps she had few friends. Hers might be a story about needing companionship. Perhaps that's why she became an amazing teacher, still able to be touched by young children reaching out to connect with her.

Arguing for Stories

Living the narrative life is about embracing the stories that make us who we are. The traditionally academic way to explore this issue would be to prove that the stories shape our personalities. I might draw on the work of Jerome Bruner, for instance, who explores how narratives help shape our understanding of self (1990, 111–15) and how our psychological understanding of reality is formed through narrative modes of thought (1986, 88). Such an approach, though, is built upon a combative arrangement between the writer and the reader. This argumentative mode requires me to arrange evidence to counter any doubts one might have about my claim that stories construct us. This is an approach built around the logic of objectivist argumentation. Such an approach creates distance between writer and reader, depersonalizes. It is, in short, a nonnarrative form of writing, of seeing the world.

In place of this, I offer here an exploration of how readers might benefit from telling their own stories. I attempt to enact this exploration by telling a real story I've taken from my own life. It is my hope that this approach will engage readers in a real desire to begin recording their own stories as I try to show how powerful such acts can be. Thus, what I am attempting to do here is take a narrative approach to the problem of convincing readers to value stories. I want to use stories to argue that stories are worth arguing for. There are already so many academic books that celebrate essayistic life, the cool, objective life of science. I offer, in contrast, then, a narrative approach to life. I offer a story about why we need to tell stories.

Who Am I?

As a kid, my world was full of dangers: poison ivy, loose gravel that would skid a bike out of control, oversized schoolyard bullies, mothers with plates of vegetables, girls' slimy kisses. To battle all these evil demons, I used to carry around a wooden shield. The shield was made of sanded pine, smooth and cool to the touch. It was perfectly round, twelve inches in diameter, and had a small wooden handle on one side. I had used crayons to color alternating red and white circles from the outside of the shield to a one-inch ring at the middle. In the very center of the shield I had drawn a white five-pointed star on a circle of blue. The shield was, I felt, an exact replica of the one Captain America used when he joined the Avengers (Lee 1963). The only flaw in my shield was one tiny hole near the outer edge. This hole had been a spout through which had been poured the contents of the barrel that the shield had originally covered. Unfortunately, that hole tended to limit the effectiveness of my shield for stopping bullets the way Captain America's did, but the hole did give me a good handhold for slinging the shield at bad guys.

That one comic book I had bought on Maxwell Street Day had sprouted into a modest collection by the time I was ten. I used to carry all my comic books in one oversized, heavy-duty plastic bag with white plastic handles that would snap shut. In those days I didn't worry about keeping my comics in mint condition. I just liked to read them, over and over. That was how I spent the summer of 1979—reading comic books. My parents had just bought seven acres of land in the country. My father, who was a professor but had once been a carpenter's apprentice, was building a new house for us. He and the professional carpenter he had hired worked on the house all summer. My brother spent each day watching them and pounding in the occasional nail. I sat on a canvas deck chair about twenty yards down the hill, in the shade of some oak trees, just at the edge of the sound of the hammering. I didn't care about building things; I just liked to read.

Of course, that was partly because I was clumsy and uncoordinated. I had been hit by a car when I was six, had broken my leg, and though the injury had healed, I was never any good at sports after that. I remember once bragging to my mother that I had finally beaten one of the girls during the six hundred–yard dash, so I didn't come in last; my mother burst into tears when she heard my story. Small wonder, then, that I lost myself in a world of superheroes. Captain America had been a scrawny kid, too, before volunteering to be injected with the super soldier serum that made him powerful. Spider-Man was a geeky bookworm before a radioactive spider bite gave him superhuman powers. The fantasy world of superheroes was a place where shy, unassuming guys like me became the center of attention. And it was a world where it didn't matter if you were smart, either. Iron Man built his own supercharged suit of armor to protect his heart and to fight evil. Ant Man was a scientist who fought crime using his own inventions. Batman had no powers at all other than his brilliant mind!

In the comic books, the story of how a superhero gets his power is called the origin issue. But if I wanted to tell my own origin story, as the Professor, one version would surely be grounded in my reading of comic books. Unfortunately, most English professors don't wear cool costumes or fight much crime besides plagiarism. Nevertheless, the world of comic books that I entered through reading taught me to value the world of fiction. Before long, I was writing my own comic books, too. The Crime Killers, a group of superheroes who looked very much like D. C. Comic's Justice League, was my favorite invention. They had all kinds of battles, from the middle of the Pacific Ocean to the Sahara Desert. From there, I was soon reading the mythologies of the Greeks and Norsemen, writing my own myths, seeing *Star Wars* and reading science fiction, and finally devouring the classic Western canon, from *Moby Dick* to Shakespeare. My life trajectory into double majoring in English and journalism in college, working as a technical writer, and then pursuing a doctorate and teaching position in the field of composition were all in some ways linked to my early exposure to comic books.

Yet even more than that, because I began my literary education not with the classics but instead with comic books, I've also maintained a sympathy for and interest in alternative forms of representation. Thus my valuing of narrative expression over the more widely accepted academic discourse of the field is in some ways the result of how my childhood literacy story unfolded. My love of comics, an often-derided art form, has caused me to find value in alternate discourses in the face of damning outside judgments. I have, I suppose, grown accustomed to being a literary outsider. Of course, this form of othering pales besides more serious forms of discrimination, yet the othering is still both troubling and identity-shaping for those who experience it. In his memoir, famed writer Stephen King talks about the shame associated with the genre of writing he loves, the horror story. Consider his comment on the subject, for example,

> "What I don't understand, Stevie," [Miss Hisler] said, "is why you'd write junk like this in the first place. You're talented. Why do you want to waste your abilities?" . . . She waited for me to answer—to her credit, the question was not entirely rhetorical—but I had no answer to give. I was ashamed. I have spent a good many years since—too many, I think—being ashamed about what I write. (2000, 49–50)

Reflected in this quote is a common concern about the way certain discourses are othered. Like little Stevie, I heard the same thing many times from my parents and teachers about comic books: "Why are you reading that trash?" My father even limited me to buying one comic book a month and required me to read novels from an approved list of classics as well. Only years later, when comic books began to accrue high value as collectibles and *Spider-Man* became the fifth-highest grossing film of all time, earning $403,706,375 at the box office (Yahoo! Movies 2003), did I feel my interest in comics had earned a bit of dignity. But as King says, the feeling of shame lingers on.

Living the narrative life, then, means learning that who you are is all about the stories that form your life. Both my career as a composition professor and my love of alternate discourses began as far back as 1973 when I roamed Platteville's Maxwell Street Day with a nickel in my hand. My beliefs, my values, my tastes, and my biases are all linked to the stories of my life. And thus, as I write my own story, I come to understand better what motivates me, what drives me, what predisposes me to certain kinds of philosophical stances. Not that I can shake off those stories: my love of comics, which has led to my amassing a collection of some five thousand books, won't go away. But, in retelling those stories, I can see how, for example, my teaching has been affected: if I allow students to write fantasy stories in an introductory composition course or grade a science fiction story highly for creativity, I am looking to reshape the academic world into a place where I would have fit. I'm resisting becoming Miss Hisler, resisting calling any literary genre trash. I am, in effect, trying to honor the stories that made me who I am. Living the narrative life means never closing the book on your own stories.

Preserving Your Past

"The struggle of man against power is the struggle of memory against forgetting" (Kundera 1986, 3). The past slips farther from us each day: names, faces, the way sunlight bounced off a pool of water just before you dove into it. Kundera points to the more alarming ramifications of memory loss: the way control of the world is altered by those who tell our history. It is easy to see the truth of Kundera's claims if we look to the way politicians make one claim while running a campaign and then act as if they had never said such things when it comes to their actions in office. Consider, for instance, that when George W. Bush campaigned for United States president, he ran as a candidate who could bridge partisan gaps, going so far as to say in his presidential acceptance speech, "I was not elected to serve one party, but to serve one nation" (Wagner 2000). Three years into his presidency, Republicans and Democrats were bitterly divided and Bush's spokespeople no longer mention bipartisanship as a goal of his administration.

On a practical level, however, the grand stories of national and world events seldom work their way down to our lives in specific ways. We can complain about presidential politics or shed tears over national tragedies, but then we go on living our ordinary lives. So while we might vow not to forget, as political critic Michael Moore (2002) does when he says, "Al Gore is the elected President of the United States. He received 539,898 more votes than George Bush" (2), we really can't do much to directly rewrite the story of our nation. Even voting doesn't seem to count, or be counted, for much these days.

Far more important, I would argue, than our frustrations over distant problems are the real incidents and events that make up our lives: birthday parties, a first kiss, the loss of a loved one, taking a walk in the moonlight. Some of these memories, of course, stay with us forever. But too many fade despite how much we might wish to hold onto them. It's especially easy to see this when one thinks of close friends who have slipped from acquaintance as time and distance have intervened in life. Peoples' names and faces last for a while, but many of the good times slip away. Telling our own stories is one way to hang on to these memories, to preserve the details, to save and treasure things that really mattered to us.

———

Like the time Dave, Steve, and I were walking back from a Burger King run. It was during final exams week at the University of Wisconsin and Burger King always ran these one-dollar Whopper specials. So we'd each eat two or three Whoppers, not even bothering with French fries because the burgers were cheaper.

And then on this night, as we got back near the dorm, Dave said, "Why don't we climb that wall?"

We told Dave he was nuts, but Dave said it was the kind of thing a superhero would do, and since we were all comic book collectors, we decided it was a challenge worth tackling, no matter how risky. The wall was maybe twenty feet high and went up at a sloping angle. It was made of large boulders that offered plenty of handholds. The fall would have hurt, probably would have led to someone literally breaking a leg, but it was a manageable climb, and so the three of us set off. The first few feet were pretty easy, and Dave and I moved up quickly. We were a little more fit than Steve, who had to pull himself harder, but we all were managing the climb. But then, about two-thirds of the way up, I felt my arms start to shake a little. I got nervous, then, and it seemed I couldn't find any more handholds.

"I'm going back down," I said. "This is stupid."

"Oh, come on, Gian," said Dave. "We're so close now."

And Steve said, "You can't quit, Gian. This is our one chance to be superheroes."

And then the fear passed and my hands calmed down, and I pulled up over the last few feet. Dave caught my hand at the top, and we were there, towering twenty feet above Ogg Hall's parking delivery area.

All that was left to do then was for the three of us to do our secret handshake.

Taking risks, conquering fears, defining friendships: we can preserve all of these when we record our stories. The stories might be silly or serious, epiphanies or mistakes. The point is, these stories belong to us. They're not delivered by a television. They're not canonized by some literary critic. The simplest stories are often the ones we treasure most, and so they're the ones we need to write down, either to share or just to save, but always to make sure we don't lose them.

Elsewhere I have written about the value of narratives for preserving history, the value of creating narrative accounts of important events, such as the 1997 Teaching in Cyberspace Through Online Courses (TicToc) Symposium. In my article "The TicToc Story," I discussed why it was useful to write a story about the events of that symposium: "to preserve a historical record of the event; to preserve some of the thoughts and ideas that existed during this short moment in time; to provide, through narrative, alternative ways of understanding the TicToc project, ways perhaps more intuitively or emotionally based; to help readers connect to the people and the spirit which was/is TicToc" (1997, 46).

The Pulitzer Prize–winning writer Tim O'Brien (1990b) considers it vital that we use stories to preserve the lives of the people we meet. He argues, in fact, that our lives depend on such stories:

> But this too is true: stories can save us. I'm forty-three years old, and a writer now, and even still, right here, I keep dreaming Linda alive. And Ted Lavender, too, and Kiowa, and Curt Lemon, and a slim young man I killed, and an old man sprawled beside a pigpen, and several others whose bodies I once lifted and dumped into a truck. They're all dead. But in a story, which is a kind of dreaming, the dead sometimes smile and sit up and return to the world. (255)

Writing down our stories can even help us remember events that were lost. I had completely forgotten my treacherous climb up that rock wall until I began this section. But now the story has come back to me, and it is preserved here. In this case, it's a story that might not matter much to anyone but me and Dave and Steve. But my hope is that as this story is read, it will jog other people's memories. We each have stories of friendship, special times we wouldn't trade for gold. I've just found one of those stories from my life and, I hope, now I'm not alone.

Living the narrative life means learning that our stories matter and, therefore, wanting to record them.

Developing Narrative Sympathy

I remember my first comic book so well because before I could buy my second one, a car hit me. I was walking home from first grade. I was maybe a block or two from Hamner Robbins School. A few of my friends were on the other side of the street, and they called me to come over. So I looked, quickly, and darted out between two parked cars. Then I found myself lying in the street with people talking to me, and I was calling for my mom. My lunch box, an orange and blue Hot Wheels lunch box, did make it to the other side of the street, where someone found it, smashed in on one side. It's a shame, about the lunch box; it would be worth a small fortune now.

I wound up in the hospital for what seemed like ages. They put me in a body cast because my left leg was broken. I don't remember the operation or the pain, the smells, or the noises. What I do remember is being in the hospital ward, in a high bed with stiff white sheets. The T.V. had a remote control. It was a little beige box with a couple of buttons and a long black wire that ran up to the back of the T.V. I liked to just hold the button down and listen to the channels click by one at a time. I may have been one of the first people to ever channel surf.

Sometimes I had the ward to myself, but there were a few other beds in there, and the nurses moved people in and out of there from time to time. I spent forever in that hospital ward: months and months. Years, even. I was six. My mother would know how long I was really there. But it wasn't far short of forever.

At one point, a teenage boy got assigned to my room. He was tall and thin with dirty blonde hair. His arms looked a little scrawny from what I could see of them. The sad thing is, I don't even know what his name was. I suppose I learned it and just forgot. What I do remember, though, is that this kid was a comic book collector. He had tons of comic books, a bunch on his bedside table and some more in a box by his bed and tons and tons at his home. So the kid and I would talk and flip through the T.V. channels and read comic books. I remember he had issue number 145 of *The Fantastic Four* in which the Human Torch and Medusa fought Ternak in the snowy netherlands of Antarctica. I read that comic book with amazement. We both had a good time. I seemed to make him laugh a lot.

The kid had leukemia. It hurt like hell. Every night he'd start screaming in pain, and I would wake up scared and press the black call button for the night nurse. But she would never come. The kid would scream and scream, and I would press and press the button. Then I would just start shouting for someone to come help us. Then it would pass and he would lie there quietly for a while. The room would be dark with just a little light coming in from the hall.

"Are you alright?" I asked one night. "Is the pain gone?"

"Who's your favorite superhero?" he said in reply.

"I don't know too many," I told him. "Batman, I guess. He has a pretty neat costume."

"Mine's Professor X. He's this bald guy who's in a wheelchair. He doesn't wear a costume. He can't even walk. But he's got these mind powers. He can do all kinds of stuff with his mind. Blast people and read their thoughts."

"That'd be cool," I said. "There are a few people I'd like to blast."

"Yeah, he's powerful. He's got his own superhero team called the X-Men. And he can do all sorts of things. Even though he can't leave his wheelchair."

We lay there, then, in the darkness. Maybe the nurse finally came. Or maybe I fell asleep again. Or maybe we just waited in silence. It didn't matter. Before long, the screaming started again.

In the mornings, a woman would come by the hospital rooms with a cart that had candy and toys and flowers. There were comic books on it, too, and so the next time my mom came for a visit, I asked her to buy me *The Fantastic Four* comic my friend had let me read. He wasn't in the room at the time, probably gone to therapy or somewhere. When he got back, he said, "Why'd you buy that? I would have given you my copy."

"Oh," I said. "I didn't know that."

A few days later, the kid left the hospital. He said he was going back home. And then he put a big box of comics on the bed and said I could have them all. So I wound up with two copies of *The Fantastic Four*. And my friend? My mother told me people with leukemia often didn't live very long. But I liked to imagine that he had gone off to a secret lab somewhere and been injected with a new drug that not only cured his leukemia but also gave him never-before-seen superpowers. So, he's off fighting crime somewhere and using his powers to do good.

Telling your own story sensitizes you to the stories of others. Sometimes that's a burden. The real story, of course, is that they sent my friend home to die with his family. They couldn't treat his leukemia. And he ran out of time. My mother said she sent his family flowers because he was so nice to me and it was so sad for a teenager to have to die like that.

There are lots of people in our stories: good guys and bad, tragic characters, and mysterious personages. When we tell our own story, it reminds us that we're not alone, that we depend on others to help us along the way, to reach the happy endings. My friend needed stories. He needed to know that there were people like Professor X who could get beyond their wheelchairs, reach beyond their illnesses. And I needed my friend's stories: the stories in his comic books, of colorful heroes and wild adventures and evil villains, and the story in his head, of a boy dying of leukemia who reached out with a box of comics and passed on a treasure. These shared stories made us friends. That was all either of us could ask for or give. Stories connect us to other people, and we have a responsibility to respond to those stories. In his book *The Call of Stories*, the psychologist Robert Coles (1989) talks about how his mentors helped him learn the value and necessity of these stories. One of his mentors was the famous physician and poet William Carlos Williams, who put the lesson this way: "Their story, yours, mine—it's what we all carry with us on this trip we take, and we owe it to each other to respect our stories and learn from them" (30). Living the narrative life means answering the call stories impose.

Celebrating Me

I've been teaching composition for twelve years, and every semester a few students ask me if they are allowed to use the word *I* in their papers. Why English teachers ever got into the habit of banning words rather than celebrating them, I'll never understand.

Taking away the word *I* is the same as taking away someone's power of speech. Certainly, people can write documents to instruct and inform others. But if there is any real value in the act of writing, it is in how we use writing to teach ourselves. To live a narrative life, a person needs to understand this. When I write, I write for me: the writing helps me figure out who I am, what's important to me, what I think and know.

Donald Murray (1991) argues that all writing is autobiographical, that even if we remove the word *I* from our vocabulary, we are always writing from our own particular vantage point in the world:

> We are autobiographical in the way we write; my autobiography exists in the examples of writing I use in this piece and in the text I weave around them. I have my own peculiar way of looking at the world and my own way of using language to communicate what I see. My voice is the product of Scottish genes and a Yankee environment, of Baptist sermons and the newspaper city room, of all the language I have heard and spoken.
>
> In writing this paper I have begun to understand, better than I ever have before, that all writing, in many different ways, is autobiographical, and that our autobiography grows from a few deep taproots that are set down into our past in childhood. (66)

Even when we construct an "objective" argument, our choices have been shaped by our life histories. Murray argues that writers really have only a handful of topics, all deeply rooted in their pasts.

If Murray is right, then it's when we don't include *I* in our writing that we're wasting our time. Murray cites research by Vera John-Steiner into the importance of allowing students to pursue their private interests in their writing, even when students seem to be obsessing on a particular topic. Murray sees this as highly valuable because such personally focused writing helps students come to terms with issues that are troubling them. In fact, Murray argues that we need to let students do more of this sort of writing, not less:

> I do not think we should move away from personal or reflective narrative in composition courses, but closer to it; I do not think we should limit reflective narrative to a single genre; I do not think we should make our students write on many different subjects, but that they write and rewrite in pursuit of those few subjects which obsess them. (73)

I, I, I—is this a turning inward, obsessive nihilism, an overnarrowing of our gaze? Perhaps. But we have only one pair of eyes. We're always locked into our own worlds. Placing myself into my writing helps me figure out exactly where my vantage point is, where I'm standing, where I'm coming from, and where I'm going. We've got to figure ourselves out in order to figure other people out.

Murray even argues that the reading we do is autobiographical in nature; we read about and come to understand other people's lives by interpreting these texts through the lenses of the stories we know. And artificial intelligence researcher Roger Schank lends support:

> When people talk to you, they can only tell you what they know. And the knowledge that people have about the world around them is really no more than the set of experiences that they have had. Now, of course, not every experience that someone has had is worth remembering, let alone telling to someone else. The experiences we do remember form the set of stories that constitute our view of the world and characterize our beliefs. In some sense, we may not even know what our own view of the world is until we are reminded of and tell stories that illustrate our opinion on some aspect of the world. (1990, 29)

Schank's research focuses on trying to create computers that can think like people. And to do that, he tries to build computers that can tell stories. Schank says that our minds store information in the form of stories that we can retrieve for later use:

> What makes us intelligent is our ability to find out what we know when we need to know it. What we actually know is all the stories, experiences, "facts," little epithets, points of view, and so on that we have gathered over the years. . . . When our experiences come to mind, we can adapt them to a new situation if we are problem-solving, reduce them to a one-liner if we are in a short conversation, or tell them whole if we have an interested listener. We can compare two stories and attempt to find the similarities and differences, or we can alter a story to invent a new one for some purpose. . . . Knowledge, then, is experiences and stories, and intelligence is the apt use of experience and the creation and telling of stories. Memory is memory for stories, and the major processes of memory are the creation, storage, and retrieval of stories. (15–16)

Schank's work helps us see how our own stories help us make sense of the world. We figure new things out by calling to mind stories that seem related. We try to understand things that are different for us through the lens of things that are familiar. In short, we have to find some way to write ourselves into the story if we want to understand it. The essayist Adam Gopnik explores the motivations of writers who retell other people's stories in his article "The Story of Us All." In this case, Gopnik examines Alice Randall's *The Wind Done Gone*, which is a reworking of Margaret Mitchell's *Gone with the Wind.* In *The Wind Done Gone,* Randall replaces Mitchell's hero, Scarlett, with her mulatto half sister, named Cinnamon. Gopnik argues that retelling such a story is not simply about trying to provide a critique of the original work or even a more equitable account. Rather, he says, the urge is more emotional:

> The whole let-me-tell-you-what-they-won't craze, in fact, seems to have started back in the sixties. . . . This suggests the human emotion behind the literary artifice. The desire is not so much to deromanticize the romantic classic . . . as to make a new romance in which somebody more like you does the romancing. What bugs the rewriters is the unchallenged existence of somebody else's romantic narrative, the other guy's or girl's romance. . . . Naturally, we want to vote them off the island—and vote ourselves onto it. The impulse behind "The Wind Done Gone" is not to create the world as it was; it is to create a cinnamon Scarlett worthy of a cinnamon Rhett. (2001, 37–38)

While Mitchell's estate sued to try to prevent the publication of *The Wind Done Gone,* Gopnick applauds this notion of rewriting a story from your own point of view. In fact, he says, it's the only way to fill in missing gaps:

> And why shouldn't we cast ourselves in the big parts, make literature into a kind of po-mo karaoke? . . . Writing always leaves something or someone out, after all, and those who have been excluded can reach for the pen and tell it for themselves. As you read this, it is already being rewritten from the point of view of the author's children, whose clamor for lunch is left unheard; the online programmers, whose agency in getting it to the office is left unseen; and the copy editor, who invisibly fixes its grammar while sighing at its small ironies. They have their stories, too. (37–38)

What Gopnick is arguing for, the retelling of stories from our own point of view, is, in fact, what Schank argues our minds do automatically. It just becomes clearer when someone puts it into print.

When I was a kid, growing up in a small rural farming community in Wisconsin, I used stories in this way to understand people who seemed very different from me. I wrote myself into stories, either literally, as I wrote my own comic books, or in my imagination, as I pictured myself as a character in the comic books I read. And so I would become a super-powered mutant, someone whose DNA was different from the rest of the world, someone whose genes made him powerful but also a freak. In these stories, I learned what it meant to not fit in, to be different from everybody else: "Allow me to introduce myself. I'm Professor Charles Xavier. You're at my school for gifted . . . for mutants. I solicit their admission so I may help them learn to deal with a world that hates and fears them" (Macchio 2000, 13). I became one of Xavier's X-Men, and I battled supervillains and also racism and bigotry, fighting to protect the same people who were disgusted by my difference.

The fact is, we need to be part of the story. We need to tell what we know. We need to use the word *I*. Living a narrative life means beginning with who you are. Telling your own story. Celebrating me. It's a beginning, a place from which to figure things out. It doesn't mean the whole world is focused on me, that I can't understand anything or care about anything except myself. It means I learn to understand and to care through the stories I hear and tell. I get to you through me. I'm in the story, and in the end, so are you.

Finding Your Way

The world is a hard place. It's full of crime and corruption. It's a place where teacher pay is low and business executive pay is obscenely high. The world is subject to violent terrorism, economic downturns, and ecological pollution. At the same time, our world can be so dazzling. Wake a half hour early some morning, and an orange glow will cut through the darkness as you rub your arms against the cool of the morning. Go to bed a half hour late and a glittering of stars will spot the dark blue of the night sky while crickets rattle your ears. Eat lunch with a friend. Watch a baby learning to laugh.

Sometimes the whirl and stress of our working lives makes us miss all this, both good and bad. We look no further than our desk or the next hour. In her book *The Working Life*, scholar Joanne Ciulla (2000) discusses the problem:

> One of the great ironies of modern life is that we live longer but we seem to have less time, because we have more things to do. In her book *The Over-worked American*, economist Juliet Schor describes how work hours have been increasing over the past twenty years while leisure and vacation time have decreased. According to her estimates, the average employed person in America worked 163 hours more in 1987 than in 1969. Women average 305 more hours of work than they did in 1969. The amount of free time fell nearly 40 percent since 1973, from twenty-six hours a week to slightly under seventeen . . . downsizing often forces workers to put in longer hours, and few complain to their bosses, because they fear losing their jobs. (171)

Ciulla explores the many pressures of working life, particularly the shift of income away from workers and toward executives and alterations in business economics that have made management manipulation and downsizing routine. In the face of the depressing nature of the business world, Ciulla says,

"The way we think about work, leisure, and the way we live depends on how we see the big picture of life. On a day-to-day basis most of us deal with decisions about our lives ad hoc, sometimes losing sight of what is important to us. We know that work can make life miserable or rewarding" (207). She says we are faced with answering for ourselves what the meaning of life is and how that meaning impacts our work life: "meaningful work is something that we have to find on our own" (226).

Ciulla, of course, does not offer any simple answers to such grand questions. Nor will I. But I do believe that leading a narrative life can help us find our way. In this chapter, I've taken you back to when I was a little boy busily reading a sign that said, "COMIC BOOKS FOR SALE—ONLY 5 CENTS." I've explored how narratives can teach you about yourself, how they can preserve your past, how they can sensitize you to the stories of others, and how they can focus your understanding of the world from a personal vantage point. But there is one more thing stories can do.

I'm out for a walk one day late in September. There are leaves in the street and I'm wearing a jean jacket to keep off the cold. But I can feel the sun starting to warm things up, and so I'm walking quickly, headed to the first big hill on First Street. And then I see a "Garage Sale" sign with a red arrow pointing down a side street. I'm ahead of schedule anyway, so I follow the sign.

The garage and the driveway of a yellow house are loaded with stuff. There's an old couch and a few lamps, a stair-climbing machine, and some toys. A rope strung from two highchair backs holds hangers with dresses and shirts. Some boxes are filled with odds and ends. There's even a stereo with a turntable and an eight-track cassette player.

I spend some time looking around. A few people are browsing. One woman is haggling over the price of a round wooden mirror on a two-foot stand. I examine a push lawnmower, but it is old and dirty and doesn't look to have many lawns left in it.

Then I make my way into the garage by stepping over a pile of old tools and a red rake leaning on a garbage can. The garage is dark and there are more boxes here with clothes and kitchen gadgets, a toaster and a blender and a coffeemaker, cups and plates and silverware. Someone has sorted through his or her life, clearing out the junk, getting a fresh start.

In the back of the garage, I find what I'm looking for: two tables piled with paperback books. I start to sort through them when I spot two young boys crouched just to the left of the books, digging through a box of comics.

"Just pick one," says the bigger boy.

"I can't pick," says a tiny boy in a gray Elmo T-shirt. "They're all so good."

"Come on, Phil; Dad's waiting for us."

Phil keeps flipping through the books. A stack of seven or eight comics has been placed to his side. He adds two more two it.

"Phil! Come on."

Phil's brother has his comic in his hand, *Moon Knight*, the hero darting across a rain-swept building in his black and silver costume, his cape billowing behind him.

I squat down beside the two young boys. "Anything good in here?" I ask.

"Yeah," says the older boy. "There's loads of good stuff." Then he leans closer to me and whispers, "Don't tell anybody, but this *Moon Knight* is worth four dollars in my collector's guide."

"Really?" I say. "Better not bend the cover." I turn to the other boy, then, Phil: "What are you buying?" I ask him.

"I can't decide."

"What about Batman? He's a pretty cool hero."

"I have some of him already. There are too many. I can't pick."

"Hmmm," I say. And then I know what to do. I reach into my pocket and get out my wallet. "You know what?" I say. "This does look like a really good box of comics. So here's what we're going to do." I hand the older boy a twenty-dollar bill. "That ought to be enough for the whole box. You guys can split them. But let Phil have the first pick."

Both boys stare at me.

"Here," I say. "Tell your dad somebody bought me a box of comics once too."

"Wow," says Phil.

They both thank me and the two of them drag the box toward the front of the garage. I walk out a side door, tell an older woman in a lawn chair to have a nice day, and head back to the street and my walk up the hill.

I believe that stories can guide us. Certainly, they can help us figure out right from wrong. But the stories don't have to be religious in nature. Sometimes, all we need is to remember the story of someone's good deed, someone's act of kindness. That's what happened to me that fall day.

I think, as well, stories can help us when we truly aren't sure which way to go at all. When we feel the most lost and confused. Consider this: During the Vietnam War, Tim O'Brien is trapped in a firefight above a field that turns out to be a village's outdoor sewer (since the village has no indoor plumbing). It is raining while the soldiers are being shelled, and the field below them turns to swampy quicksand. O'Brien's friend, Kiowa gets sucked into the swamp, and though O'Brien tries to save him, Kiowa is pulled under and dies. O'Brien blames himself for not having the courage and strength to save Kiowa. Few of us can imagine how we would cope with such a tragedy. We're fortunate to be spared that. But O'Brien had to find a way to move on. For him, stories became the answer. Stories helped him find his way again:

> I did not look on my work as therapy, and still don't. Yet when I received Norman Bowker's letter, it occurred to me that the act of writing had led me through a swirl of memories that might otherwise have ended in paralysis or worse. By telling stories, you objectify your own experience. You separate it from yourself. You pin down certain truths. You make up others. You start sometimes with an incident that truly happened, like the night in the shit field, and you carry it forward by inventing incidents that did not in fact occur but that nonetheless help to clarify and explain. (1990c, 179–80)

Stories help O'Brien keep going, past the devastation of war and loss. He uses them to save himself and to save, as well, the friend he couldn't save in life.

To live the narrative life, then, is to open yourself up to the possibilities of stories, to give yourself over to them, to trust them. Stories are a kind of magic. Simple magic, really, but magic all the same. If we tell our own stories, preserve them, study them, we can find in our stories some of the answers for which we're looking. I'm sure not every war veteran can face the horrors of war through stories, but it's clear stories have helped O'Brien. And I'm certain many other soldiers, and other people, have been helped by stories as well.

PART FOUR

Ruota's Graveyard

At the back of the graveyard we find the pictures of Alesandro Franconi and Annunziata Barsochi. Small round frames, the pictures yellowed by years of Tuscan sun. The Italians mark their dead this way. Not just a name and a date, but a real face, my great-grandmother's, her skin white and wrinkled, a black bonnet wrapping her head, and eyes that did not see their way down from this Pisa mountain.

Ruota's graveyard is at the edge of the village. A gray stone path at the side of the church leads to it. The graveyard is on a hill, 36 feet by 60 feet, about the size of a small backyard. A low stone wall surrounds the place, and the gate is held open by an old piece of red string. Inside, the graves sit neatly on either side of a thin concrete walkway. There is a small shed, as well, in the middle, with a padlocked door and a couple of rusty buckets. On the left side of the shed, slabs of marble, two or three to a stack, are propped up. They are not needed yet.

"Here's another 'Pagnucci,'" my wife calls to me. "Bar-la-mi-no. He was born in 1875."

I walk over to her, read the headstone. Barlamino's wife was Eufemia Landini Pagnucci. She outlived him by 20 years. A small bunch of yellow flowers, still fresh, rests by her name.

"And this must have been their daughter. Michelle." My wife, Edel, points at the next grave, a black-and-white stone, and the letters still a bright gold.

From Ruota's graveyard, on a hilltop in Northern Italy, the view east is of small towns with bright roofs. I try to make out the places I know: Luca, Altopascio, Castel Vecchio. But everything looks the same. Miles of open grass and winding roads, fields of sunflowers, and the orange tops of Italian homes.

The wind blows Edel's hair as we stand looking. To the south it is all trees, evergreens mostly, and I point out the spot where my grandfather still owns land, just up a ways from the road.

We have begun recording the names in a little notebook:

Margharita Pagnucci

Angelo Pagnucci

Carola Pagnucci Natali

Francesco Natali

Luigi Natali

Luigi Mei

Eni Barsochi

Vincenza Mei

"They're all related," I say, waving my hand at the whole graveyard.

"Just a few more rows here to write down," says Edel, "and that corner by the gate. We started over there, by your uncles, remember?"

"Alright then, but we won't take down all these Guerras. Tommaso, here, he only married a Mei. It looks like the rest of his family didn't mix with mine."

I leave Edel writing down the names and walk over by the shed. One of the marble slabs is cracked, and I see that it is not a blank headstone, as I had thought, but already carved. I move the cracked slab to look, and they are all old headstones, the writing faded but still legible. There is no room for them, I guess, these stones. It is a small graveyard after all, and crowded. On the ground behind the shed I find another tombstone in the grass, but this one is so worn I cannot read it.

Eventually we get them all. All the Mei sisters who married Paolinis and Lupettis and Barsochis. Romolo Pagnucci, who was a priest. Carolina Mei

Pagnucci, my other great-grandmother. Her husband, Francesco, who died in 1949.

We take pictures of the pictures. We straighten the flowers, tossing the dead ones in a corner. We find an old candle, half melted. We put it on top of the largest headstone in the place, Erina Di Ercole's, and Edel finds a match in her bag. The candle flickers for a bit, but there is too much wind, so eventually we give up on the idea.

Then two Italian women come walking up the church path. One is carrying a garden spade. The older woman says something to us, but we don't understand.

"Americani?" she asks.

We nod.

The women have come to tend things. So we pick up our bags and the list of names and leave the graveyard, on a hillside, in the sunlight.

Your Mother

Imagine

> if she *didn't* tell long stories
> > about your childhood

> or hug you
> > every time she saw you

> or cry
> > at weddings

> or mail you
> > boxes of candies
> > that have been *hand* stamped with love

> or forget
> > who likes Texas sheet cake
> > and who *hates* it

> or tell you
> > she's *sure* having fun

> or make you
> > do the dishes and clean the house

> *or*
> > had joined the Peace Corps
> > > instead of marrying your father
> > > because he sat with his tie
> > > in his coffee cup
> > > and made her *laugh*.

Telling Family Stories

My father came to America when he was nine years old. That was in 1949.
He learned English playing with kids on the street. In Ruota, the mountain
village where he was born, nobody went to school much beyond the third
grade. But everybody knew that in America you got ahead by going to
school. So my father went to St. Charles Military Academy. It was an all-
boys school, and he was studying carpentry. He even had an apprentice-
ship with a local carpenter. It was good money. That's what you did in
those days, you went to school and you learned a trade. That's how you got
ahead. At least, that's what a poor Italian immigrant family thought you
did to get ahead.

For them, that was enough. In Italy, they had had nothing; once while
still there, my father and grandmother even had to split an egg between
them for a meal. In America there was plenty to eat, and schooling led to
good-paying jobs. What more could you want?

Forming Cultural Identities

Pursuing the narrative life will lead you into your family history. Italian, Irish,
Brazilian, Japanese, or Nigerian: family stories have already constructed us all.
They impact how we look, what we eat, how we move our hands when we
talk, how we think about the world.

Earlier, I mentioned Neil Postman's "Learning by Story," but his work is
also relevant to the importance of family stories. Postman writes, "Human
beings require stories to give meaning to the facts of their existence" (1989,
122). We use stories to make sense of our worlds, and those stories are normally first told to us at home by family members. Exceptions exist, of course,
but the majority of people have some sort of family whose member(s) begin

the first work of teaching us how to understand our world. Postman says we use these stories we learn "as moral and intellectual frameworks. Without such frameworks, we have no way of knowing what things mean" (122). Of course, family stories are heavily shaped by the culture we live in. Postman is very aware of this, saying we derive many of our critical meaning-making stories from "the more profound stories that people, nations, religions, and disciplines unfold in order to make sense out of the world" (122). In short, the stories we learn as children from our family members are stories of identity and ethnicity, they are the stories of our various cultures.

Postman cites two such examples of what he calls "profound stories," one dealing with the United States, the other with the Soviet Union:

> In America we have told ourselves for two hundred years that our experiment in government is part of God's own plan. That has been a marvelous story, and it accounts for much of the success America has had. In the Soviet Union they have told themselves a different story: that their experiment in government is history's plan. And in seventy years their story has transported them into a position of worldwide importance. (122–23)

Postman says these stories have become outdated with time, but it is easy to recognize their current replacements. In the war with Iraq, President George W. Bush certainly told the American people a story when he explained how American military might was being used to forge a new world order.

Postman sees such profound stories, then, as a way for nations or people "to provide themselves with a sense of continuity, or identity" (123). Stories help us define who we are. They give our lives a sense of meaning. As Rosen points out, "strip us of all the accumulation of stories heard and told, reported and invented, traditional and spontaneous, and what is left of us?" (1986, 8).

Writing Family Story Albums

Over time and hopefully as we experience educational growth, we often come to question at least some of the grand narratives of our cultures, to ask, for instance, why God would bless *only* the United States or why any benevolent divinity, for that matter, would write a story for just one nation. At the same time, though, these profound stories and also the smaller but equally important stories we've learned from our families, stories such as how we are to behave, what we should seek to be happy, what is meant to entertain us, all of these stories reverberate in our minds for years to come.

Most of us use our holidays to return to our families and retell these stories. Weddings, funerals, new baby nieces and nephews, these are moments not only to see the people with whom we have blood ties, but to relive the stories that make that blood flow.

> *Then one day a shop teacher noticed young Gianfranco Pagnucci. This kid was really bright. What was he doing in a shop class? He ought to be in a college prep program. I don't know why the guy decided to help my father, but he sent him to a guidance counselor who helped my father get a college scholarship. That eventually led my father to a teaching career and the publication of seven books and over two hundred poems. That was all it took, just a moment of insight by one observant teacher who realized building was just one of many things for which my father had a talent.*

Now this family story has been with me for a long time. In some ways it's an inspiration. An Italian kid who couldn't speak a word of English at the age of nine grows up to be an American poet. My father didn't just learn to read and write a new language, he mastered that new language in perhaps its most intricate form, poetry. This was my father's personal story of the American dream. It was the story of how our family made it in the world.

So imagine my surprise one day when I picked up Mike Rose's *Lives on the Boundary* (1989) and read the same story. An Italian kid in a remedial track gets noticed by a teacher, gets switched to a college track, and eventually becomes an excellent teacher and an expert writer. The details of the two stories are different, but the dream part is the same: Italian kids grow up to be American writers. The two lives share the same story line.

Families tell such stories over and over to support themselves, to give themselves pride. Mothers, especially, love to do it. Ask almost any mother what her children were like as babies, and you'll get a long list of their many great accomplishments.

And even if we cringe when we hear our mothers' stories—"not that old story again"—such stories also have shaped who we have become, who we are. Stories of pride teach us about our potential. Negative stories can be just as powerful, creating children full of self-doubt. Either way, the stories of our families make us into the people we will eventually become. These family stories are important, then, because of how they shape our view of the world, how they inform what we try to accomplish with our teaching, how they direct what we do with our lives. We might be following in a parent's footsteps, becoming a teacher like our mother, or resisting our parents' lives, swearing never to view the world as they do. Either way, the stories of our families serve as powerfully constructive forces on what happens to us, who we become. Ann Green (1999) puts it like this:

> I spend a lot of time when I'm teaching trying to remember where I am, where I come from. The question of where I am has a lot to do with who I am; my family likes to stay in one place and has, for the last one hundred and fifty or so years. So when I think about the stories that I tell about my teaching, they are connected to place, to the literal politics of location that determine where students and I are, how I read their writing, and how they read me. I am a heterosexual white woman from what can sometimes be called a "working-class background." (18)

Green's pedagogy is critical/feminist in its approach. She works to help students expand their level of critical consciousness by challenging both their and her own comfort levels. At the same time, she says, "Sometimes when I write, I remember the other people I might have been if circumstances were different" (21). In her chapter, Green explores how her responses to a student's paper that discusses race are impacted by Green's own background. She struggles with her own sense of identity as she works to help her students excavate categories of race, class, gender, and sexual orientation from the inside out. To do this, Green also has to wrestle with her own family history, which has constructed her understandings of such categories.

Bob Mayberry (1999) states outright the impact of his family on his identity. Like so many fortunate children, Bob's mother read regularly to him as a child, shaping him into a highly literate individual. Frank Smith's *Joining the Literacy Club* (1988), among other works, makes clear the importance of family influence on literacy development. Mayberry, though, takes this notion of parents reading to their children and places it into exactly the right sort of story framework to guide us back to our own memories of being read to as children:

> My mother sat across the table from me, day after day, and read aloud while I ate. What I remember is steaming tomato soup, but she couldn't have served that every day. I was in the third or fourth grade and walked home for lunch, across the empty playground—everyone else ate in the cafeteria—and down the dirt path that wound through a dairy farm until it came upon the backyards of the tract houses of our neighbors and, next to last on the path, our metal gate . . . coming home for lunch each day was pure pleasure—I never missed catching the gate in one, perfect swing, CLANG. . . . A perfect lunch for a perfect swing of the gate: steaming tomato soup, a sandwich, maybe some canned pears or applesauce, and

milk with a cookie or two or three. It's what I fix myself today, nearly forty years later, when I'm sick or depressed or simply need to recall the pleasures of life. (1999, 118–19)

In a delightful article, Mayberry shows how family and lunch constructed his belief in the value of literacy, contrasting it nicely with his experience reading Dick and Jane basal primers at school. In fact, because Mayberry found school to be boring, he argues that his mother had a much more profound impact on his learning:

> My mother was the most influential teacher I had. She read to me . . . [*The Adventures of*] *Tom Sawyer*, made certain I could read and write before I began school. My learning habits, especially the crucial habits of reading and writing, were shaped by her, my writerly identity forged in a kitchen filled with the smell of soup. She taught me to appreciate the pleasures of the text. (120)

Family stories keep us warm. That, and tomato soup.

Responding to Tragic Family Stories

Unfortunately, of course, not all family stories are as warming as Bob Mayberry's. Stories of family feuds and hurtful incidents abound, sadly, and sometimes these conflicts prevent the story from making the potential connections I have suggested. Most of us know fathers and sons who haven't spoken for twenty years, cousins who weren't invited to weddings, family black sheep. Stories, in fact, have a destructive power that can keep such feuds alive. Bitter moments live on in our memories and in our retelling of these unhappy narratives, making the harm last and last. And the worst stories, of abuse and injury, some of these can't ever be untold, even with years of therapeutic retellings.

Yet, sometimes, as we retell even the worst stories, those of family members who had to suffer greatly, such as in times of war, the telling of these stories is the only thing that can bring any sort of healing. Gil Haroian-Guerin (1999) discusses this when she writes about her grandmother's experiences living through the genocide of Armenians in Turkey before World War I, a genocide that Haroian-Guerin says took nearly two million Armenian lives (4). Horrible times often cause those who endure them to put up a wall of silence, to attempt to block out and forget the past. In addition, the children of such survivors, Haroian-Geurin says, often encourage this silence, mistakenly thinking it is better for the survivor to move on and not dwell on a wretched past:

The children of survivors experience much anger, love, and confusion at their emotionally scathed parents. Many cannot bear to read any accounts of the survivors for this reason. A few cut themselves off from Armenians. On a spring morning in June, does anyone want to hear the histories like my grandmother's or hear my Aunt Eva's[?] (10)

Haroian-Guerin, though, is convinced that encouraging silence only causes greater harm. She believes survivors need to tell their stories if they are ever to know any sort of real healing. Haroian-Guerin says that the cost of silence turns families into "emotional ovens" (11). And so, she says, families, both survivors of tragedy and their children and grandchildren, must "keep talking, keep writing, for words do break the silence. Only these acts of writing and telling can break the spell of anguish and agony. If we do not come to terms with the past, we are stuck in it" (11–12). Denying one's history, one's family stories, is perhaps the most terrible thing of all, Haroian-Guerin concludes: "If a rare few did manage to deny their Armenian identity altogether, they discovered the worst fate of all: to be free-floating particles in this universe, isolated humans with no roots, no context, no history, no room of their own" (12).

Caring for a Family Tree

I once asked my father why he became a writer. This is the story he told me:

> *St. Charles Academy was a Catholic school. Lots of Italian kids went there, and many of them had trouble with English. My father, though, just took to the language. It was a gift. The nuns even used to say to him, "It's wonderful you can write so well." Excelling in English, then, became a sign that he had truly assimilated into American culture. "If you could write English well," he told me, "then you really knew you had become a good American."*
>
> *Soon my father was even writing on his own outside of school. He began to write poetry, quickly becoming a skilled wordsmith. By the time he finished two years of work at St. John's University in Minnesota, he had become known as the Lord Byron of campus because if a guy got into a fight with his girlfriend, he would have my father write a poem to smooth things over. It was not long after that my father would turn this skill into a career, as an English teacher, helping other people learn to write.*

If you want to live a narrative life, sooner or later you'll be drawing your family tree. It's a common grade school activity. I think I was in fourth grade when my teacher asked us to make a family tree. I jotted down my parents' and my grandparents' names and figured that would cover it. My mother made me put a little more time into it. She got me to add my aunts and uncles and got me at least to go back as far as my great-grandparents. By that point, I had run out of space on the worksheet, so then I *really* knew I was done.

Unfortunately, though, I don't even have that meager bit of genealogical research at my disposal anymore. It was tossed out along with my Captain America shield, my wooden army trucks, and my favorite book of dinosaurs. My parents needed the space and, as my mother pointed out, the dinosaur book *was* historically inaccurate. How can accuracy in a story matter when you have a great gory picture of a *Tyrannosaurus rex* eating some helpless herbivore, complete with running blood? Don't ask me. Getting the facts right always matters less to me than getting the right story. But opinions on that topic vary.

At any rate, some thirty years later when I began to try to construct my family tree in some real genealogical detail, I found that, for once, I really did want to get the facts right, but getting the names and dates quickly proved to be a challenge because so many of the people with that information had died. Unless one's family happens to have a bible with a family tree (or its own genealogical nut), most family history details never get written down. The memory resides in the minds of grandparents and aunts and uncles, who in my case don't speak English very well. This leaves archival research, including trips to county registry offices, immigration sorting points like Ellis Island, and genealogical research institutes in countries of origin. A few online resources like Ancestry.com (2003) are also quite helpful.

In response to my own struggles to reconstruct my own family tree, one thing I did was to alter my pedagogical approach to teaching my department's research writing course. Most English departments expend a great deal of effort on teaching students how to write effective research papers, devoting a good portion of a required introductory composition course to this effort, if not an entire specialized course to the topic, as at my institution. Certainly there is good merit in learning to write effective research papers, since at least one or two other college professors are likely to require such a paper in an upper-level course. So I dutifully spend many weeks on this topic, going so far as to even teach APA style in addition to MLA, believing that not all of my students will choose to major in English.

Light banter aside, when I consider how much time I have spent in life doing research on topics such as getting a student loan, buying a car, taking out a home mortgage, and finding a job, I wish my education had helped me learn to find information *besides* books in a card catalog and journal articles in an electronic database. The ability to conduct and write about research is vital, yet when those skills are limited to the creation of expository research papers, it seems much is being overlooked that our students might need to learn.

On the other hand, there isn't time to teach everything, I realize. Every teacher has to pick and choose. So, working as I do from a narrative ideological stance, what I have begun to ask in my research writing courses is for students to research their family histories. I ask students of course to make a family tree, going so far as to make them contact a parent for help in getting the tree right instead of half filling it in from memory. (The urge to fill in a worksheet as fast as humanly possible never seems to go away!)

Even more important than the work of mapping a family tree, I ask students to gather from their family members stories that are worth preserving. These might be stories the students know well, like something funny that happened at the last family reunion cookout, or things they may not know, such as how their parents or grandparents met. I also ask students to gather and scan for permanent storage important family photos. And, most challenging of all, I ask students to write a story or poem describing an important family heirloom. Students have trouble with this last task, at least initially, because they often don't have heirlooms readily apparent to them. Some students might have a piece of jewelry that's been passed down from mother to daughter or perhaps a hunting rifle that's been handed down. Some students might even have a family treasure like a painting or special lamp or handmade quilt. In many cases, though, students say their family has nothing particularly valuable that could be handed down.

It's not that surprising, I suppose, that we've reached an age where the family heirloom is becoming a thing of the past. In the United States, we're more of a transient nation now. People lose their jobs more often or move more frequently, looking for better-paying work. Families break apart more easily, relatives get spread farther apart and are seen less often. Being able to pack belongings quickly becomes more important than being able to keep them. Most of what we own becomes technically obsolete in a short time anyway. And so, my students tell me, we have nothing special from our families, nothing we have is worth saving. "Except your stories," I tell them. "Stories are the one heirloom no one can take away from you." So I tell them that, instead of a precious book or an antique chair, they should find some object in their home that has a story to tell. Those are the objects many students write about then, poems about ovens and refrigerators and television sets, stories that tell of parties and laughter, football games and fights and love. In a world without heirlooms, we make our own.

Lad Tobin (1997) talks about receiving similar stories for a collection of student materials his university published annually called *Fresh Ink*: "One of the most common genres was the highly sentimental eulogy for a beloved grandparent . . . sweet and touching tributes to the one adult who had provided the author with unqualified love and a model of how to live" (80). It's clear from his chapter that Tobin is a lover of student writing, but the enthusiasm of these family stories sometimes gets the better of him:

> Though the sweetness of the grandparent submissions to *Fresh Ink* should have provided some relief in an otherwise bleak landscape, I found the opposite to be true. Of all the submissions, these bothered me most of all. I found myself immediately impatient and dismissive as soon as I read about Poppy's favorite stuffed chair or Grammy's apple turnovers. I found myself doubting that Nanny's eyes always twinkled like a starry night or that pappa always smelled like peppermint. (80)

I admit, I've read more than my share of such stories now too. But of course there are plenty of darker stories, for those who prefer that sort of narrative, since, unfortunately, students have so many of those stories to share as well. Yet students imbue even these dark stories with a glimmer of hope. As Tobin notes about his students' submissions:

> Still, one trend has not changed. Almost all of the student submissions have happy endings. At least, that's how they are intended. After detailing a hundred ways that they have been damaged and dissed, scared and scarred, these student authors usually try in the end to put on a happy face. "Now I've learned never to take life for granted." "It's all for the best; you only learn through suffering." "But I know he's in a better place." "I'm glad my father was not like the other fathers; he's special." (82)

Tobin says critics of personal writing (he uses the term *confessional* as well) say this is one of the reasons the form is inappropriate for student writing, since "we academics crave ambiguity, sophistication, doubt, even cynicism" (83). Do we want students to grow bitter like us, to grow pale in our shadows? To his credit, Tobin comes to realize that students have no choice but to write these stories. And this is precisely the point. Good or bad, people have to tell their stories so they can move on. The larger narrative, the story that is our life, to keep that narrative going, we need to keep forging happy endings for ourselves. I would argue that, if we can't learn from suffering and have no better place waiting for us, then the narrative of our life is most likely to end in darkness or suicide. I believe Tobin's students choose to tell stories with happy endings, remember he says that almost *every* student makes that choice, because they want happy endings for the stories of their lives. We all do. I think.

So let me give you one. By the time my students are done writing their stories of eating grandmam's cookies and watching the Pittsburgh Steelers with pap, they've also completed the research on their family trees. So we all look them over and see how far back our pasts go. And then I have the students write their ancestors' names on the board: Strittmatters and Sunseris, Weavers and Joneses, Razzanos and Addeos, Mukasas, Muhamadous, Imbrognoes, Sanchezes, Gadis, and Batainehs. Names that are proud and funny and strange and impossible to say and beautiful. Names from across the globe. Names of people who worked and suffered, loved and hated, danced and wept, tried and failed and tried again. My students write on the board all the names that will fit of the people who did all they could so that one day, their sons' and daughters' sons and daughters could go to college to find that much sought after better life. And I tell my students that better life starts today, with these stories. And I believe it.

Telling the Stories That Matter

There is an extraordinary letter, in a book full of many such letters, that Michael Blitz and C. Mark Hurlbert (1998) use to try to say how vital it is that teachers find ways to make their classrooms places where the world can start to change. It's a long letter, but let me try to crystallize its sentiments for you:

> To: Our children . . .
>
> It feels strange and exhilarating to write an e-mail letter into the future. That's what this is. Not much different from the traditional, mysterious envelope that appears at the reading of a will. The heirs open the letter with shaky hands to read what the dearly departed has left them in words composed by the living hands now folded in repose. . . . You'll find this one day. . . . In so many ways, you, our children, have been our measures. What we do, we do with you in mind. . . . What will it take to do something tangible, something real that will make their paths even slightly more clear to our students? What will it take for us to do the same for you? . . . What should we do in a world that's come undone? What stories must we teach you? What stories will you tell? What reasonable hope do we have that you will survive to tell stories? What world(s) do our teachings reflect? Are any of these the right questions? We're still asking.
>
> With all our love,
> Your Dads (16–17)

Blitz and Hurlbert use their composition classrooms as places of healing for their students. They want to offer students some way to respond to the violence in the world. For Blitz and Hurlbert, that means allowing students to write about anything that really matters to them, anything that will change them, engage them, anything that they are burning to talk about to the world (8). Blitz and Hurlbert want teachers to find ways to connect education to real life: "Writing and living and teaching are not separable" (2).

If we are to do such a thing, then one of the things we must allow students to research is their own families. Life begins at home. Yet for far too long, our idea of studying and researching life has been to look elsewhere, at other, distant cultures. Earlier I discussed one of the many difficulties my doctoral students have had in getting approval from the internal human subjects review board just to study their own classrooms; I shudder to think what sort of resistance they would face if they dared to suggest conducting a research study about their own families. The fact is, in all my years of teaching, no doctoral student has ever suggested family research as a dissertation topic. A few students have written class papers about relatives' stories, mostly narratives of literacy development, but that's all. Of the dozens and dozens of research proposals and dissertations I've read, not one has focused directly on anyone's own family. In fact, only two or three doctoral students have even made passing mention of their families, and those were cases where the students were trying to explain only one dimension of the genesis of their research topics rather than the focus. These passing remarks about family, though, proved to arrest the attention of doctoral committee members. The students were questioned and criticized and challenged for having included even these small family references in their work.

Even in writing this chapter on telling family stories, I have had to look far and wide to find scholars who talk directly about their families' importance or relevance to their work. For the most part, it's just not done. Work and home are kept separate, family and colleagues are kept distinct, and the researcher's gaze is turned elsewhere. It might be OK to study someone else's family, but no one does research on his own family. It's just not a legitimate topic.

As with so many other dimensions of the narrative life, these academic restrictions, whether written or unwritten, spoken or inherited in silence, limit what we see and know. Writers like Rose (1989) and Villanueva (1993) include early chapters in their books that mention their families before moving on to more academic concerns. Both Rose and Villanueva are also telling their autobiographies. They have not set out in any considered way to study their families or to collect specific stories from them. Imagine, for a moment, what we might learn by studying our own families: husbands interviewing wives, parents interviewing children, grandchildren researching the lives of grandparents. I realize, of course, that such research raises a number of potential problems—reliability and validity questions, ethically dangerous ground. Would a husband answer his wife's questions truthfully or tell her just what she wants to hear? Would a grandchild ask hard questions about a grandparent's wartime actions? Certainly, we are unable to learn everything, and we wouldn't want to. But we can learn many important things from gathering the stories of the people we love and care about.

Writing became my father's life story, his career, his passion. But what happened along the way to the Italian kid who was at the beginning of that story? Did he disappear? Did he vanish under the weight of a new language? There was a time when my father was just a little boy playing marbles in the streets of Italy. If I had met him then, the best we could have done was said "ciao," "hello." But of course, I never met that boy. What was he like? What happened to him?

My father was twenty-seven when I was born. He'd been gone from Italy for almost twenty years by then. He was American, a mid-westerner, married to a nice girl from Elgin, Illinois. He taught English. Italy was gone. He waved it into his past from the bow of a ship. Who needed it, anyway?

My father still knows how to speak Italian, though he never does. Maybe a few words, now and then, to my grandmother, at holidays. My father can still read and write Italian, too. But he doesn't. A few times, in his poems, he might use a word, "cavallo," once, I remember, like a dead horse.[1] He wrote his master's thesis on John Ciardi, the Italian poet. And when I was ten, we went to see Rocky.[2] There's not much else, Italian, that's left. "But, we're here. It's America. Take it easy."

Except.

He wouldn't go back. Not to Italy.

"I hate to fly," he would say. "It's not safe."

My mother wanted to go. My grandparents did go, every year for a while. But not my father. Not for thirty-five years. And then just the one time.

"It was dirty," he said. "Polluted, crowded, noisy."

And there was the language, too. Italiano.

"Teach me to speak Italian," I would say. "I want to learn."

"Why bother?"

I tried anyway. I learned to say "nonno," for grandfather, and to count, "uno, due, tre."

---

1. In "A Dead Horse" from *Ancient Moves* by Franco Pagnucci, 1998.
2. Directed by John Avildsen in 1976.

"He should learn Italiano," Nonno would say to my father.
"You teach him then."
You were avoiding it. Italy. The language, the country, the past. Just say it. You were ashamed. It's OK. It doesn't matter.
"No. You're making it up. Nothing wrong, no shame, no coverup. I'm Italian. Sure. Always have been. Pagnucci. Just ask me."
And that's it, of course. The name. Always there. Every year, in school, the first day. They'd be reading the role, one name after another. And then . . . the long pause.
"It's John," I'd say. "That's how you say it. Like 'John.' It's easy. I just spell it G-i-a-n. But you say it 'John.' It's Italian."[3]
No getting around the name. It marks you. Pagnucci. Italian. Capisci? Except.
He changed it. His name.
His name is Gianfranco Pagnucci. That's his full name, but he always goes by Franco. Shortening a name isn't that big a deal, I suppose. Lots of people do it. Yet he even published a book once that only had Franco Pagnucci on the cover, a place where you would expect to see the full Italian name.[4] *Still, that's only a small thing, more of a technicality.*
But there's more. He used to call himself Frank. For years. It was easier. And he even made up a middle name for himself, since he didn't have one. Most Italians don't have middle names. So my father just picked one. Paul. That was it. For years he was Frank Paul Pagnucci.
He always wanted a middle name, he said, like his American friends, so he just made one up.
"Why not? They did it to us. When we got here. They changed all the Italian names. They were too hard to say. Your Nonno. They couldn't say his name, 'Fabio.' So they changed it. And his brother, Ivo. They changed all the names."
What can you do? We all need to fit in. Sticks and stones . . .
You know why he changed it back? The wedding. Right, that girl, from Elgin. He was Frank then, still. But, the marriage certificate. It was my grandfather, on my mother's side, he's the one who said, "You've got to use your real name. It's a legal document. You can't use a made-up name.

---

3. See Chapter 5 of *Life of Pi* (Martel 2001) for Piscine Molitor Patel's similar troubles with his name.

4. Again, see *Ancient Moves* by Franco Pagnucci, 1998.

Even an American one. It's got to be Gianfranco Pagnucci." That's mar-riage for you.

"Come on," I say. "Don't tell me that. You couldn't change your name. Not your own name for crying out loud. That's just not right!"

"Sometimes you want to fit in."

But how can I accept that? Isn't my father's name the one thing that still says he's Italian? Pagnucci. It's Italian. For sure. Italian. Cut and dried, draw a line in the sand, no doubt about it, Italian.

You change your name, even a little bit, and it's like you're cutting off an arm. You lose yourself that way. Frank is not Gianfranco, and it shouldn't be. No way, no how, never. If you're Italian, you're Italian. That should mean something. Your name should mean something.

"You do what you have to do. Times change. Things were different then. It's my name, my life. I changed the name once. I changed it back. I could do it again. And I would, if I had to."

But.

But I remember. You told me the story, the story of Ivo and the hammer. My Uncle Ivo, he worked in a factory after he came to America. It was hard, noisy work. Back breaking. But Ivo, he was tough as nails. Nothing he couldn't do. So he took the job, did his share, earned his pay. And he kept a smile on his face. Ivo, he liked to laugh and talk and joke. He was a good guy to have around, kept things easygoing. Except one day, who knows, maybe Ivo says something or makes a bad joke. Or maybe it's just one of those things, one of those days. But some guy gets pissed and calls Ivo a damn dago.

Ivo doesn't say anything. They were all eating lunch. Ivo, he gets up from the table and walks across the factory floor a ways and then bends down and picks up a hammer and throws it at the guy.

He could have killed him. He meant to kill him. Luckily, he missed and the other guy ran off. And Ivo shouted after him that he would kill him, the next time, if the guy ever came back. And he never did come back.

That's how the Pagnuccis were. They were Italians first and Americans second. They spoke Italian in their homes, cooked Italian food, and trav-eled back to Italy to see their relatives as often as they could. They were very proud to be Italians.

I started writing this story about my father thirteen years ago. I keep going back to it. Over and over. Trying to get it right. Trying to figure out what it means. I can't understand it. It's too full of contradictions and prob-lems and emotions and tensions. It's about who I am, who my family is, who the Pagnuccis are. I suppose I've really been trying to figure this story out my whole life.

In his novel *Atonement*, Ian McEwan (2001) explores our need to sort out the story of our life, the bewilderment and even panic we can feel when that story begins to unravel or slip beyond our comprehension:

> It was in his clear moments he was troubled. It wasn't the wound, though it hurt at every step, and it wasn't the dive-bombers circling over the beach some miles to the north. It was his mind. Periodically, something slipped. Some everyday principle of continuity, the humdrum element that told him where he was in his own story, faded from his use, abandoning him to a waking dream in which there were thoughts, but no sense of who was having them. No responsibility, no memory of the hours before, no idea of what he was about, where he was going, what his plan was. And no curiosity about these matters. He would then find himself in the grip of illogical certainties. (231–32)

I'm arguing for telling family stories because I believe they hold the key to the things we need to know. But maybe I'm wrong. Maybe, after all these years of working on this story about my father and my Italian relatives, maybe there is no making sense of any of it. Maybe I'd be better off with a neat and tidy five-paragraph essay, a contained thesis. Stories always have so many blasted loose ends, so many pieces that contradict the argument you thought you were trying make when you started to write them.

Then, just when I'm about ready to chuck the whole thing, I stumble across a copy of Tom Romano's *Writing with Passion: Life Stories, Multiple Genres* (1995). Reading the first chapter of his book, "Truth Through Narrative," my breath catches when I come across a section where Romano mentions that his daughter, a high school senior working on an English paper, "had chosen to research Ellis Island and 1914, the year my father, then a boy of nine, immigrated to the United States from Italy" (8). Romano, of course, is Italian; like me, the son of an immigrant father. I know a kindred soul when I find one, *un paisano*.

Romano tells us the story of his father's immigration as it has been narrativized by his daughter, Mariana. We see the family story through her eyes:

> "Felice felt he was drowning in the ocean of people," she read. "He closed his eyes and tried to breathe. He could feel the small wooden pony against his heart and remembered Luca. Tears welled in his eyes but he swallowed them this time. Giuseppe would call him *bambino* again and hit him. Felice wanted to be strong too, and he wanted to be able to stand up to Pap like Giuseppe said he was going to." (9)

Romano says that the story Mariana writes is a crucial means for her to come to know and understand her family history. Romano puts it like this:

> In her short story Mariana explored a mystery she'd been aware of for years—the great influence on our lives of my father, he dead then twenty-five years, the mythlike story of his family's immigration to an America decades away from designer jeans, fast-food restaurants, and alternative rock music. She conjectured in her fiction, too, inventing detail, action, and characterizations that had not been documented in family stories but that carried the illusion of reality nevertheless. (9)

Mariana's story helps Romano relearn his own family history. She gives him a new vision of his past:

> I'd never imagined my father as a boy at the moment he arrived in America, never imagined that he may have left a best friend in Italy, that his sister may have slept and his younger brother may have cried. Because of "The Wooden Pony," Mariana's fictional dream woven of image and story, language and imagination, I would never think of my father in the same way again. (10)

Is it the answer to my own questions about my family stories? No, of course not. Nothing is ever that pat and easy. I wouldn't want it that way. But Tom Romano and his daughter Mariana help me see the kindred search for our ancestral past. We want to know what it was like, what they went through, how a grandfather or an uncle or an aunt came halfway across the world to make a new life. What it cost them, what it meant to them. We want to know that story because it belongs to us. It's our family's story. And it's the telling and retelling of the story that matters, using fiction as much as fact. Mariana's story is, as her father says, conjectured, a blend of the real and the imagined. But Mariana doesn't have to get the facts right to get the story right. Tell it and retell it. That's the answer. Share in the story, enter it, merge their lives into the narrative of your own life. Become *famiglia*.

> *And so, I go back to the story, one more time. Did my father have to give up some of his Italian pride to become an American writer? Yes, I'm sure he did. Every word he wrote in English was just one more word he didn't write in Italian. Each English word carried him just a little farther from his heritage. But who could blame him? He was good at English. Even the nuns told him so. We can lose our past, Italia, without even knowing it.*
>
> *How many immigrant children go through that loss? How many give up the story they've always known for the story we've offered them instead, that magical and unreachable story, the American dream? Most people*

would say that to prosper in a new country, perhaps just to survive, one needs to learn that country's language. However, that kind of knowledge has a price. As we teach kids to write in our world, I wonder how much they lose touch with their own. When we help, or sometimes force, young Italian, Russian, or Spanish kids to learn English, we aren't just educating those kids; we're changing them. I think that's probably what happened to my father. Learning English changed him.

Except.

Except that change and loss are a part of life, a part of the story. The Italian story is just as much a myth as the American dream. What story am I after, in the end? What is it I want? To make my father forever that little Italian boy, walking through the olive groves on the Pisa Mountains?

If I asked him, I imagine my father would say that he is a poet at heart, and he would have been a poet whether he was writing in English, Italian, or even Chinese. We all make sacrifices as we go through life, and if he lost some of his Italian identity along the way, well, he didn't lose it all.

"It was all a long, long time ago, Gian. But don't worry; I still have the stories. I won't forget."

And then, from a drawer of his dark oak desk, he'd pull out a small sheet of paper, a few lines of poetry, to remind me that we can't let go of our family stories, even if we want to. Those stories are in us, to the bone, as distinct as the look of an Italian face:

The Nose

pointed,
not bent,
down,
toward the earth,
as it should be.

—*Gianfranco Pagnucci*

Storied Wisdom

"Jesus Christ, it's against the *rules*,"
Sanders said.
"Against human *nature*.
This elaborate story, you can't say,
Hey, by the way, I don't know the *ending*.
I mean, you got certain obligations."
(Tim O'Brien, *The Things They Carried*, 1990d, 122)

Through stories the mundane can become momentous.

Readers want stories. Postmodernism is dead, consigned to the museum of academia where it belongs. It's one of the reasons why American cinema, for example, has always been so strong. Stories about ordinary people tend to be appreciated by ordinary people, and, oddly enough, stories about tweed-jacketed sociology lecturers and their laconic therapists tend to be appreciated by nobody at all. The same is true for novels. People want to read stories which inform their lives, which bring news from the world of the writer to the world that the rest of us inhabit. Readers want to know what it is like to be someone else for a moment, so that they know in some profound sense what it is like to be themselves. This is the miraculous power of fiction, the power which Keats called the sympathetic imagination.
(Joseph O'Connor, *The Secret World of the Irish Male*, 1994, 146)

Brent then said that humans are the only animal able to feel the pain of sorrow that has been stretched out through linear time. He said our curse as humans is that we are trapped in time—our curse is that we are forced to interpret life as a sequence of events—a story—and that when we can't figure out what our particular story is we feel lost somehow.
(Douglas Coupland, *Life After God*, 1994, 223)

I heard a story like that once.

> *"Bub, it's all right,"*
> *the blind man said.*
> *"It's fine with me.*
> *Whatever you want to watch is okay.*
> *I'm always learning something.*
> *Learning never ends.*
> *It won't hurt me to learn something tonight.*
> *I got ears," he said.*
> (Raymond Carver, "Cathedral," 1989, 222)

Hey, what's your story?

Stories are representations of a negotiable reality. Told as they always are, from particular perspectives, they are interpretations of reality, or what Foucault would call "fictions," particular ways of shaping experience in terms of particular values and concerns. . . . Stories, as an important potentially empowering form of speaking and writing, are more than just tools for individual imagination and self-discovery . . . for teachers and students stories are at the heart of the social and political transaction that constitutes teaching and learning.
(David Schaafsma, *Eating on the Street: Teaching Literacy in a Multicultural Society*, 1993, 48)

That story must have been the bane of Luke's life.
(Mary Lawson, *Crow Lake*, 2002, 8)

This book introduces a theoretical framework for studying narrative fiction. A *narrative* recounts a story, a series of events in a temporal sequence. Narratives require close study because stories structure the meanings by which a culture lives. Our culture depends upon numerous types of narratives: novels, short stories, films, television shows, myths, anecdotes, songs, music videos, comics, paintings, advertisements, essays, biographies, and news accounts. All tell a story. This definition of narrative provides the central premise of our book: The events making up a story are only available to us through telling.
(Steven Cohan and Linda M. Shires, *Telling Stories: A Theoretical Analysis of Narrative Fiction*, 1988, 1)

That's a helluva story.

I tell this story, at least partly, to ask a question. Who *is* the narrator of the personal essay? Postmodern theory has put great distance between the self who writes and the self in the text, between empirical experience and its discursive representation. . . . However, when students self-disclose, they do not see their narrational *I* as a fiction. They believe they are describing events as they experienced them. In fact, labeling as fiction the personal narrative could cause a student to feel that he or she is not being believed; such disbelief could retraumatize the writer . . . we should respond to that personal narrative with great sensitivity, a sensitivity that is informed by a belief that the student is trying hard to describe the past or present self and relationships as that student currently sees them.
(Karen Surman Paley, *I Writing: The Politics and Practice of Teaching First-Person Writing*, 2001, 205–6)

No one knows the story I'm about to tell you.

The [sixth-grade] children . . .
knew that they were rejects in the school,
and they also knew that the school as a whole was a reject. . . .
As soon as everyone was settled I began as directly as possible and asked the class
what books they wanted to read.
Naturally they asked for sixth grade readers.
I told them I felt the books were too hard and they groaned.
"We're not so dumb, Mr. Kohl."
"I won't do that baby stuff again."
"Mr. Kohl, we can read anything."
I asked the children how well they thought they read and they became confused;
no one had ever told them. They only knew that every year they got the same
second- and third-grade books, which they knew by heart. My first lesson
became clear. I took out the class record cards and dumped them on my desk.
Then I explained to the class what grade reading scores meant, and what
the significance of IQ was. . . .
"Let's see what these cards say."
There was suspense in the room as I listed the scores:
IQ's of 70, 75, 81, 78 . . .
then anger.
"Mr. Kohl we're not that dumb."
"It's phony."
"No one taught us that stuff, no one ever told us."

But they knew now. After a heated debate I threw my first question back
at the class.
"Tell me what books you want to read."
The class chose fifth-grade books, ones they knew would be difficult for them in
preference to ones that were on their supposed "level."
They were ready to fight to read and learn, met my challenge,
and kept on challenging themselves and me for the rest of the year.
(Herbert Kohl, *Thirty-Six Children*, 1988, 184)

We never get the same story twice.

... why have so many writers
chosen to confine themselves
to the limitations of the first person
when literature is the one place
you can choose to be God?
(Patricia Hampl, "First Person Singular," 2000, xi)

The study of narrative does not fit neatly within the boundaries of any single
scholarly field. ... Story telling, to put the argument simply, is what we do
with our research materials and what informants do with us. The story metaphor emphasizes that we create order, construct texts in particular contexts.
The mechanical metaphor adopted from the natural sciences (increasingly
questioned there) implies that we provide an objective description of forces
in the world, and we position ourselves outside to do so.
Narrative analysis takes as its object of investigation the story itself. ...
Nature and the world do not tell stories, individuals do. Interpretation is
inevitable because narratives are representations. ... Human agency and
imagination determine what gets included and excluded in narrativization,
how events are plotted, and what they are supposed to mean. Individuals
construct past events and actions in personal narratives to claim identities
and construct lives.
(Catherine Kohler Riessman, *Narrative Analysis*, 1993, 1–2)

Let the story go.

I never got the chance to run away. I was too late.
He left first. The way he shut the door; he didn't slam it.
Something; I just knew: he wasn't coming back.
He just closed it, like he was going down to the shops,
Except it was just the front door and we only used

The front door when people came. He didn't slam it.
He closed it behind him—I saw him in the glass.
He waited for a few seconds, then went.
He didn't have a suitcase or even a jacket,
but I knew.
(Roddy Doyle, *Paddy Clarke Ha Ha Ha*, 1993, 280)

. . . between the activity of narrating a story and the temporal character of human experience there exists a correlation that is not merely accidental but that presents a transcultural form of necessity. To put it another way, time becomes human to the extent that it is articulated through a narrative mode, and narrative attains its full meaning when it becomes a condition of temporal existence.
(Paul Ricoeur, *Time and Narrative, Volume I*, 1984, 52)

I opened my journal, clicked my pen,
and wrote my response to narratology:
"Theories . . . theories . . . and theories
ABOUT stories, but NO stories."...
We lived in a world that did not trust them.
Stories were not true. Stories were not reliable.
If we wanted to keep stories in our lives,
we had to convert them to something else.
Something more serious. More scientific.
(Joseph Trimmer, *Narration as Knowledge: Tales of the Teaching Life*,
1997, ix–x)

[In the chapter] I related my experience of getting tenure at Michigan with a study that explored the life story of Esperanza, a Mexican street peddler. I did so not to treat our struggles as equivalent but rather to show how different I am from Esperanza, because I had attained the privilege (indeed, not without struggle) that allowed me to bring Esperanza's story across the border. I also reflected on how my Latina background affected my university's decision to grant me tenure. . . .
  It is precisely this chapter, which upsets the academic critics, that has brought so many readers to my ethnography and made them want to listen to a Mexican peddler's life story. I have received several letters from women and men who say that relating my own story made the whole book for them.
(Ruth Behar, *The Vulnerable Observer: Anthropology That Breaks Your Heart*,
1996, 14–15)

But the other reason women wanted daughters was to keep their memories alive. Sons did not hear their mothers' stories after weaning. So I was the one. My mother and my mother-aunties told me endless stories about themselves. No matter what their hands were doing—holding babies, cooking, spinning, weaving—they filled my ears.

In the ruddy shade of the red tent, the menstrual tent, they ran fingers through my curls, repeating escapades of their youths, the sagas of their childbirths. The stories were like offerings of hope and strength poured out before the Queen of Heaven, only these gifts were not for any god or goddess—but for me. . . .

I carried my mothers' tales into the next generation, but the stories of my life were forbidden to me, and that silence nearly killed the heart in me. I did not die but lived long enough for other stories to fill up my days and nights. I watched babies open their eyes upon a new world. I found cause for laughter and gratitude. I was loved.

And now you come to me—women with hands and feet as soft as a queen's, with more cooking pots than you need, so safe in childbed and so free with your tongues. You come hungry for the story that was lost. You crave words to fill the great silence that swallowed me, and my mothers, and my grandmothers before them.

(Anita Diamant, *The Red Tent*, 1997, 3)

He had the look of a man who had run out of stories.

. . . applying story-analysis methods and displaying the findings they generate moves the discussion of interviewing beyond the boundaries set by the traditional approach. . . . Looking at how interviewees connect their responses into a sustained account, that is, a story, brings out problems and possibilities of interviewing that are not visible when attention is restricted to question-answer exchanges. . . . a general assumption of narrative analysis is that telling stories is one of the significant ways individuals construct and express meaning.

(Elliot G. Mishler, *Research Interviewing: Context and Narrative*, 1986, 67)

**Which took me back
to that wonderful word: *story*.
It seemed to me at an early age
that all human communication—
whether it's TV, movies, or books—
begins with somebody
wanting to tell a story.**

That need to tell,
to plug into a universal socket,
is probably one of our grandest desires.
And the need to hear stories,
to live lives other than our own
for even the briefest moment,
is the key to the magic
that was born in our bones.
(Robert R. McCammon, *Boy's Life*, 1991, 33)

PART FIVE

Graduate Studies in Composition & TESOL
Department of English
Indiana University of Pennsylvania
Indiana, PA 15705–1087
August 11, 2002

Dear Class,
I decided I would write you all a letter as a way to bring closure to our narrative group's work for this semester. So I grabbed the best book I've read recently, *Mirrorshades: The Cyberpunk Anthology* (1986), and turned to John Shirley's story "Freezone" because it has been resonating with me of late. I think, in one of the wild leaps of meaning making which Frank Smith (1982) says is how we need to read, that much of our own explorations of narrative theory are caught up in the lines of this story. Here's a passage from near the beginning of Shirley's story:

> Rick Rickenharp stood against the south wall of the Semiconductor, letting the club's glare and blare wash over him and mentally writing a song. The song went something like, "Glaring blare, lightning stare / Nostalgia for the electric chair."
> Then he thought, Fucking drivel.
> And he was doing his best to look cool but vulnerable, hoping one of the females flashing through the crowd would remember having seen him in the band the night before, would try to chat him up, play groupie. But they were mostly into wire dancers.
> And *no fucking way* was Rickenharp going to wire into minimono.
> Rickenharp was a rock classicist. He wore a black leather motorcycle jacket that was some fifty-five years old, said to have been worn by John Cale when he was still in the Velvet Underground. The seams were beginning to pop; three studs were missing from the chrome trimming. The elbows and collar edges were worn through the black dye to the brown animal the leather had come from. But the leather was a second skin to Rickenharp. (142)

You see, Rickenharp, like most of us teachers, is on his own, trying to find his way in a confusing and often disturbing world. And, like us, Rickenharp is a writer, so he is doubly isolated. Oh sure, he's a member of a band, but as the story will later tell, they don't want him. Before long, Rickenharp is kicked out and running for his life. Which has me thinking about collaboration. It's amazing, when you think about it, that we would ever find ourselves thinking, "But students don't like to work together. I don't like it. I've had bad experiences with group work." I mean, why? How? How did we ever learn not to want to work together, not to look for help? We don't need Bakhtin (1981) or Vygotsky (1986) to tell us we are social beings. We know that in our bones. How would our lives, let alone our stories, have any meaning without other people? But there's Rickenharp, on his own, leaning against a wall. So there must be, there are, forces that push us apart, keep us from working together. As teachers, we have to resist those forces. I don't think it's enough, actually, just to require collaboration; somehow, we have to teach students how to *prefer* it. It's also why it was so important that we spent one day working with those kids from the high school enrichment program, the Next Step Program (2002), that tries to help poor kids find a way to go to college. I know for some of you that day seemed too distantly related to the narrative theory content of our course, and maybe it was, but at the same time, I think that day was actually the most important of the whole semester. How many times do eight teachers get to teach in the same class? Never, in my experience. And yet, for me, that was one of the best teaching days I've ever had. Imagine if that were the rule and not the exception, if the story of teaching were one of group effort rather than of isolation.

That's the political dimension of our narrative work, the ideological dimension. One more aspect of it, anyway. If we can cast our critical eyes at the ways we like to work, the ways we've been taught to work, the stories we've been told about how work is supposed to be, then we must ask, again, who benefits from our tastes, our preferences, our values? Whose stories are we being asked to believe? What don't we accomplish because we can't keep the band together?

But of course, like most things we do, it's all hard work. There Rickenharp is, trying to write a song, and all he can come up with is drivel. And he knows it. Our stories always get the better of us. They're hard to control. We try to write them correctly, try to look cool, but nobody pays attention, someone's always doing it better. Most experienced writers know this. They write despite that fear, maybe because of it. Our students, though, we have to help them because they often feel that all they can do is produce drivel. That's why we have to support their voices, encourage them at every opportunity. So we have to watch the messages we send. How many circled grammatical mistakes equal drivel? How many low grades and critical comments equal failure? Or, the more subtle signals, when we say something and the student interprets the comment to mean that what she or he thought was wrong, an interpretation a student might never even tell us about. For all our discussion of Jeanne Henry's book *If Not Now* (1995), there's one thing we didn't talk about. What happens when a student picks up a course syllabus and sees, not just a chance to pick a book, but that the teacher has already, somehow, picked a book the student actually read for fun somewhere else (preferably on a beach somewhere)? What would a student learn in that moment? What happens when students find that their stories are also our stories?

Of course all of this is leading to that beat-up old leather jacket Rickenharp is wearing, his second skin. Our habits protect us. There's nothing better than pulling on your best T-shirt or a favorite piece of jewelry or a pair of worn old tennis shoes. And that's OK. We ought to rely on the things we know, the things we've learned that work: The old, reliable stories that we know by heart. But that reliance comes at a price, too. For Rickenharp, wearing that leather jacket cuts him off from everyone else in the bar. He thinks he's fine the way he is. And maybe that's true. Or maybe he would be happier as somebody else, *with* somebody else, even wearing a different jacket. It is *just* a jacket, after all.

So let me leave you, not with advice, but with my own story. I used to worry about my teaching. I got extremely nervous, not just the first day, but most days. All the eyes were always on me. Being a teacher was hard work. So I gave up that job. I quit worrying about teaching, quieted my nerves, and moved out of the line of sight. I made teaching more fun, and the work *seemed* lighter. In my classes, my students began to learn to read and write by actually spending time reading and writing, not just listening to me talk. And for every story I did tell, I asked my students to tell me at least two stories in return. That's what we do now, mostly, trade stories, looking for the best ones to learn from. No tricks, no secrets. No fancy teaching methods or special textbooks. Just a world of stories. The funny thing is, people actually enjoy classes like that, which makes them fun to teach. Why? Because people love stories. Stories are how we understand the world. Stories are what make us tick. But then, you already knew that. Why else would anybody write a song in their head while leaning against a wall in a crowded bar surrounded by loud music? Rickenharp's song is just one more story, and he's trying to write it, perfectly, so that we'll be able to hear the song, his story, hit just the right note. For that to work, we'll all have to listen.

Ciao,
Gian

Notes

On my floor is a rainbow of notebooks.
Yellow, red, orange, green, blue, black,
10 and a half inches by 8,
120 sheets,
college ruled,
3 section dividers,
pictures of movies or football teams
or University logos.
Good buys at 5 for a dollar.
The wire spirals slant and the covers fray
and I am forever putting things down
for later.

Telling Work Legends

In their seminal 1990 article on educational narrative research, "Stories of Experience and Narrative Inquiry," F. Michael Connelly and D. Jean Clandinin made this call for the collection of teachers' stories: "We need to listen closely to teachers and other learners and to the stories of their lives in and out of the classrooms. We also need to tell our own stories as we live our own collaborative researcher/teacher lives" (12). Some years later, these scholars offered a more detailed exploration and guidebook to doing teacher-based narrative research: *Narrative Inquiry: Experience and Story in Qualitative Research* (Clandinin and Connelley 1999). Thomas Barone (1992) makes a similar call when he says, "I suggest that we adopt an empowering view of ourselves as willing and able to educate the public through powerfully crafted, accessible stories about schoolpeople and the conditions under which they live and work" (15). In response to and/or agreement with these calls, a number of excellent teachers' stories have been written. Some of the best include Freedman's (1990), Haswell and Lu's (2000), Miller's (1990), Rose's (1989), Schaafsma's (1993), Trimmer's (1997), Villanueva's (1993), Winston's (1997), and Witherell and Noddings' (1991). While not all these teachers might classify themselves as narrative ideologues or narrative pedagogues, their works can certainly be read as in alignment with and sympathetic to the narrative way of life.

As the list indicates, there are a number of these works, and my list is certainly not exhaustive. Nevertheless, if one were to compare this list of narrative teacher research with the entire volume of educational research of the last dozen years, it would be clear that my claims about the underrepresentation of narrative accounts are true. A simple perusal of any major publisher's educational research catalog will back me up on the general scarcity of narrative-focused texts.

Still, with this solid body of narrative teacher research on hand, I wondered, when I came to this chapter of the book, whether there was anything left for me to say.

A Stack of Old Journals

I even considered dropping teacher narratives as a book topic for a while but thought better of that move since I realized so many of my readers would be interested in writing stories about their teaching, the central focus of their work lives. So I continued kicking around various ideas around about different classroom experiences I had seen and teaching narratives in which I had taken part. But I just couldn't seem to settle on the right story.

Faced with a moment of writer's block, I did what I often do when I can't think of anything to write: I went to look for a journal entry that might get me started. The problem was, this time I wasn't sure what I was looking for. So I dug into the closet.

Pretty soon a pile of notebooks, folders, and boxes surrounded me. When my wife walked past the study, she asked me what I was up to. I told her I'd been keeping journals for about ten years, and after a while they had started to pile up.

Most of the journals I barely remembered writing. But every now and then, I found one that brought out a chuckle.

"Look at this. This is a journal from when I started teaching."

"Here's the journal I made when we were in Ireland."

"This one's from the summer when I vowed to become a poet."

"I started this one the next summer. By then I was going to be a novelist."

"And this is that nightmare journal I had to keep for Deborah Brandt's class. Look at the size of it!"

We pored over the notes and stories and odd bits of collected wisdom; it wasn't a bad way to spend an afternoon. By the time we were done, I had sorted the journals into six major groups:

- travel journals—describing trips to various countries
- creative writing journals—brimming with rough poems and stories
- reading journals—holding notes and reflections about books and articles
- teaching journals—recording my experiences in the classroom
- research journals—describing academic projects I had worked on
- personal journals—containing random thoughts and ideas

Some Journaling Trends

As I read through these various journals, certain characteristics stood out. Most obvious was the intimate nature of the entries. The journals were generally written in the first person. When people's names were mentioned, no attempt was made to explain who they were, since this knowledge was assumed. References to published works were not elaborated. The entries were addressed to myself as the intended reader along with, on occasion, a second reader who was a teacher. Even if they were shared, the primary reader for the journals was still clearly intended to be myself. Thus the journal entries tended to be open and honest, reflecting doubts and uncertainties.

Along with the intimate nature of these entries, there appeared to be two main purposes to this journal writing. One was the recording of information. The travel, teaching, and research entries all described in detail particular events that occurred. By describing them in the journals, I singled out these events as worthy for later consideration. I was clearly using the journals as a way to keep track of information that I planned to reference in the future.

The other purpose for the journal entries was the exploration of ideas. The personal entries were just that, a list of presumably interesting thoughts. The reading, teaching, and research journal entries also explored a variety of insights, in this case about the nature of education.

Beyond all this, there was an inclination in these journal entries to record events as narratives or stories. The creative writing journal entries were in either story form or poetic verse. The travel, teaching, and research journal entries also followed a sequence of events. In fact, this tendency toward narration was the one thing that seemed to bring order to the ideas in the journal entries. Without the narrative story lines, the ideas appeared to flow at random, as in the personal journal entries.

Finally, I was struck as I read the journals by how much of the entries talked about work. I had journal entries from when I was writing computer manuals as a technical writer, many journal entries from my work as a teacher, and even some entries about my work as a technological support person. There were entries on looking for work, on the annoying qualities of bosses, on the inequity of graduate student and temporary faculty pay, and on what I would do if I didn't have to work. Typical stuff, really, when one considers the huge role work plays in our lives.

A Story of Journaling

Now it would certainly take a measured research approach to get a picture of any broad trends that might emerge from the way people keep journals. What interested me, however, was the way all of this past journal writing had impacted me as a teacher, in particular as a teacher of technical writing. How did the stories I had preserved in my journals reverberate in my classrooms?

Since over the years I had found journals to be such a useful tool for learning, it should come as no surprise that I had adopted their use in all my courses. Well, all my courses except one, technical writing. That course, the most worklike course I taught, did not include any journal writing, even though in my other courses, I had found journal writing to be a highly effective teaching tool. Considering all the journal writing I had done over the years, it probably seems pretty strange that I wouldn't include journal writing as part of the technical writing courses too. It sure seemed odd to me as I sat looking at those piles of notebooks. "Just what the heck have I been doing in those technical writing courses?" I now wondered. "And why?"

Why do we teach the way we do? That's a tough question. I think too often we're not really sure why we teach the way we do. This is partly why I believe we need to explore our own personal narratives of teaching. The reasons for our approaches to teaching are complicated. They are linked to our pasts in multiple and subtle ways. Like old journal entries, the things that motivate us can be distant and nearly forgotten memories. What I would like to do in this chapter, then, is explore how my stories of working and teaching, my personal histories, have both prevented me from and guided me toward using journals in my technical writing classes. Hopefully this story is a new one, based as it is both in nonteaching work and in journal keeping. Perhaps hearing this new sort of story will encourage other teachers not only to recall their own stories of teaching and working, but also, perhaps, to write those stories down.

Teaching Technical Writing

I teach at a midsized university in Pennsylvania. I get a range of students in technical writing. In the past I've taught students majoring in engineering, criminal justice, and agriculture. Now I'm teaching safety science majors and computer science students. Sometimes I'll get a business or nursing student, even the occasional English major.

While the majors of my students may change, their concerns do not. These are upper-level students. They are serious and work hard. They are close to finishing their college careers. They need jobs, and they want to be ready to get those jobs. They complain about our campus, sometimes, but they've learned a lot. They toss around terms like *lockout* and *tagout procedures, OSHA regulations, ergonomic surveys, MIS*, and *HTML programming*. I listen to their language, their talk about classes and internships, their stories of former students who got big-paying jobs or endless rejection letters. And I listen to their dreams: getting a foot in the door, going to graduate school, moving to Pittsburgh or New York, advancing into management. I'm lucky to have these students.

Technical writing is a tough course. "Real" writing for "real" people. It's a highly charged form of writing where readers depend on the information the writers are providing. James Paradis (1991) describes the pivotal role technical writers play in the dissemination of knowledge:

> As a technology becomes more complex, the rhetorical effort required to sort and reduce its expertise to some course of activity comprehensible to the operator-everyman becomes greater. As the differential between expertise and common sense becomes greater, or as the audience itself becomes more diverse, the demands made upon the operator's manual increase. We have enough information in our daily environment to operate simple tools like hammers or to carry out basic procedures like mailing letters. But with processes associated with more complex technologies and social institutions—whether computers or the filing of taxes—we require additional support. . . . We now need specialists, technical writers and editors, who can anticipate these problems and who can apply rhetorical strategies to achieving operational coherence and simplicity. (258)

Our society depends on technical writers. My computer, my lights, the air conditioner rattling in my living room as if it is ready to die—technical writers help bring these technologies to me. They explain technologies to us, helping us understand. They serve as our interpreters of the language and laws of technology.

That's a lot of responsibility. Paradis explores this issue, describing the legal ramifications of two poorly written operator's manuals. He shows how negligent writing in the manuals can be linked, at least in court, to several serious worker injuries and even one death. Paradis makes it clear that technical writing is not a job to be taken lightly.

"What if you can't describe a process sufficiently? What if you make a mistake? What if you forget something? What if the boss asks you to lie?" I ask my students these questions. A lot depends on the answers. Technical writing is serious work.

Is there room for journal writing amidst all this heavy responsibility? In the beginning, at least, I didn't think so.

My Working Days as a Technical Writer

I used to work for a little writing company in Wisconsin called The Software Resource Publications (TSR). We wrote computer manuals. Six other people worked there when I first started. Two former English teachers ran the company. Their idea was that all you needed to write good manuals were good writers.

So we worked freelance for insurance companies, car manufacturers, advertising firms, and even a cereal company. We had more work than we could keep up with, actually. Mainly we would take old manuals that were poorly written and revise them into documents that were user-friendly.

We had a little office in the basement of a small building. It had once been a dentist's office, but now it held six computers and enough desks and tables for a team of writers.

I enjoyed working there. We'd stand around drinking coffee and chatting until we were ready to write. Then we'd work all morning and eat lunch together in the conference room, or go out somewhere if we had time. Then it was back to the computers for another four or five hours of writing.

I did a lot of writing at TSR. Most of the manuals we wrote were about two hundred pages long, and usually we'd be working on two or three at a time. We'd receive all sorts of software, some of it still in a developmental stage, and we'd have to try it and then figure out how to describe it to its potential users. Sometimes we'd go visit the companies where the software was being made to interview people about how they would use these computer programs.

By the end of the day I would go home and collapse on my couch or catch a movie. I didn't keep any journals or do any writing in my spare time in those days. Working as a writer for eight or nine hours a day consumes any interest you have in writing during your free time. The last thing I could stand to do after a day of technical writing was pick up a pen.

I also never did any type of journal writing connected with my professional work. Journal writing was not seen as a part of the technical writer's job, at least not among the group of technical writers with whom I worked. If anything, we were so busy trying to get all those computer manuals written, we simply didn't have time to do any journal writing. About the closest I came to journal writing was filling out a weekly time sheet of the hours I was billing our clients. But journals in any typical sense never became a part of our working context.

Since some professional writers have discussed their use of journals (Dillard 1989; Stafford 1987), it may seem odd that professional technical writers wouldn't make use of journals in doing their work. To understand why journals weren't used at my technical writing firm, it may be useful to recall the three main characteristics I pointed out about my collection of journals. The first was that all my journal writing was very intimate in nature, usually written for myself as the audience. This is in stark contrast to the computer manuals I worked on. All the manuals were written for some outside audience. At times I even interviewed these users to find better ways to communicate with them. I think the personal nature of journal writing did not fit well with the social nature of technical writing work. When a person spends all his time trying to write for others, it seems less appropriate to write only for himself, and so journals didn't appear to make sense in the technical writing office.

In a similar vein, while I always wrote my journals individually, most of the writing I did at TSR was done in collaboration with other people. We generally had at least two writers working on each manual. Often I would have to write one chapter for someone else's manual or add a few pages to one of his or her chapters about a new feature that had been added to the software. At other times we divided up the work among three or four writers. All this collaboration could have made the manuals incoherent as they jumped from one writer's voice to the next. To avoid this problem, we all strove to write using what we called our company voice, a friendly, yet professional style. In contrast, in my journal writing, I was always striving to develop my individual writing style. So again, the technical writing atmosphere did not seem right for journal writing.

The other two traits common to my journals were the recording of information and the exploring of ideas. Now computer manuals certainly do contain a wealth of information, but this information is not a historical record of events. In addition, much of the information I recorded in my journals was either in the form of a narrative or was listed at random. The information recorded in the manuals was generally organized as lists of procedures and was highly structured. A journal might actually have worked well for keeping track of technical information. Unfortunately, because the loose structure of a journal is so far removed from the rigid structure of a manual, the idea of keeping a journal did not arise.

Likewise, computer manuals rarely contain the playful explorations of ideas that journals often do. Instead, the manuals are written as a means of disseminating factual information. This is in line with Paradis' observations about the role of the technical writer in society. Making creative insights is not explicitly part of the technical writer's job. This is one more reason journals do not appear to be useful tools for the technical writer.

My purpose in recounting my days as a technical writer is to show the wide range of reasons journals were not a part of that lifestyle. To borrow from James Paul Gee's work (2001), journals were not included in the technical writer's discourse identity kit (526). At our firm, technical writing was public and collaborative. Thinking about writing in this way made the private nature of journal writing seem an unimportant part of the writing process, and so it was eliminated from that process.

My Early Working Days Teaching Technical Writing

My workplace views of technical writing followed me into the classroom. My technical writing experiences were very evident in the first technical writing syllabus I created. For instance, I had course sections on

- applying for the technical writing position;
- getting on-the-job training; and
- managing the account.

I had gone through all these stages in becoming a technical writer myself. My career started with a job search and interviews, so I thought it only made sense to begin a course in technical writing with those same kinds of technical documents: resumes, letters of application, and lists of references.

Once I had the job at TSR, I worked on simple projects and reviewed models of good computer manuals. I built the second part of my course around these same ideas: simple, basic technical writing tasks that would give students a feel for how technical writing is done. Thus I planned to have students write simple instructions, review manuals, and study page layout and design.

After being with TSR for a short time, I was given my own writing projects to direct. I quickly learned that these new responsibilities carried lots of headaches: pushy clients, unrealistic deadlines, and printing problems. I felt my students would likewise gain valuable experience from doing a major writing project, so I had them each propose a technical research study that they would carry out and then write a report for.

What was missing from all these activities and forms of technical writing was the type of personal reflective learning that students might engage in through journal writing. I was asking students to leap into the kind of intensive writing work that I had done as a professional writer. But I have already observed how that lifestyle left me no time or energy for journal writing. To the extent I tried to model my class after the work context of the professional writer, I was creating a situation in which journal writing not only was difficult to do, but didn't seem to make sense.

The final section of my course, "Looking at the Global Perspective," might have allowed the personal type of writing for which journals are particularly useful. However, since I had relegated this section to the last week of class, there would have been little time to even get a journal started. And since courses so often fall behind schedule, it was quite likely we would only have about one day to spend on this topic by semester's end.

There were many other ways, though, that I might have included journal writing in that first technical writing class I taught. Unfortunately for the students, I did not include it. Fortunately, I was capable of learning and changing over time.

A New Course Syllabus

A drop of sweat fell from my forehead to the paper in front of me. July. I turned the air conditioner back on. The heat moved back to arm's length.

I was working on a new syllabus for technical writing. I had done a lot of thinking about the course since that day I sat surrounded by old notebooks. In reading journal entries from my days working as a technical writer, I found that the story I had told myself about how one becomes a technical writer had heavily impacted my technical writing course design. In fact, the story had shaped me so profoundly that I was actually leaving out certain teaching tools, like journals, because they did not play a role in my earlier technical writer work story. Looking at those earlier stories with a little distance, I was now ready to make some changes.

I clicked a button and my Macintosh sent two pages to my printer. I looked them over, made a few more changes, adjusted the margins, and printed again.

My story of teaching technical writing had evolved with the times. My new syllabus had a slicker format and more details. Beyond this, my course plan had been impacted heavily by technology. "Web Page Design" and "Email Etiquette" came at the beginning of the course now. Computer lab time was part of the schedule. Computer disks were part of the students' required course purchases. And even one of the explicit course goals was now to help students "utilize computers and electronic forms of communication." But the biggest change was that one of the class requirements was now keeping a work journal.

If I had learned anything from my students over the years in technical writing, it was that by the time they took my class as seniors, they were smart and had extensive background subject knowledge. So I had begun to see my job as a technical writing teacher to be one of helping students tap into that knowledge, that well of stories, and to use it to their advantage. I believed that was exactly what they would need to do the rest of their lives, both as writers and as professionals. And of course I had also learned that one good way to keep track of and explore the stories students had learned was through writing a journal.

Rethinking Journal Keeping

What I've been trying to get at through all these stories are the complicated ways we come to understand a teaching method like asking students to write journals. Like everything else, journals exist in particular contexts at particular times. My own journal writing was set in a range of narratives: while traveling, while trying to be a novelist, while taking or teaching a class.

And as I've tried to illustrate, the context of all that journal writing tended to be extremely personal. This was not a public form of writing for a wide range of audiences. My journals were set in a private context that was usually entirely my own. I also used those journals for very personal ends, to explore my ideas and feelings and creativity, to create fictional stories that had my individual stamp on them.

In contrast, I've explored a few stories of my experiences as a technical writer. This was a very public context where the writing always had a wide audience. The writing was done collaboratively with individual writing styles submerged into a corporate voice. And, of course, I've noted that this was a context where there was no journal writing, nor the interest and energy for journal writing.

Given these stark differences, it shouldn't be very surprising that my initial impulses led me to create a technical writing class that contained no journal writing. My experiences at TSR taught me to view technical writing as a public act done collaboratively to convey information. My view of journal writing, on the other hand, was of a very personal act done to explore personal ideas and record personal events. Both of these views could, of course, be questioned.

Suppose I altered my view of journal writing to bring it more in line with my view of the technical writer's context. Could I envision journal writing as public, collaborative, and a means for conveying information? This might mean new kinds of journals: dialogic journals, circulating journals, workplace journals.

Elsewhere I've examined how technical writing students respond to various types of journal writing assignments (1999). But for the purposes of this discussion, let me just review some of the curricular thought processes that went into designing my initial technical writing journal assignment.

An Electronic Work Journal Assignment

When I created my first journal assignment, I tried to make it one that required my students to write publicly, collaboratively, and for the purpose of conveying information. I tried to create an assignment that matched my story of what the life of a technical writer was like. The journal entries the students had to write were obviously public since they were to be sent to other readers via email. The assignment also asked the students to convey information, first about their class projects and then about how to improve those projects. Finally, while the journal entries were not written collaboratively, they did work toward a collaborative context since they asked students to do work, coming up with ideas, that was focused on someone else's project. Here's a short excerpt from that first journal assignment I gave to my technical writing students:

> A journal is primarily a place to work with ideas. That's how we will be using journals in this class, as a way to push our thinking. And while many journals are private, we'll be sharing this writing so that you can bounce your ideas off other people. Thanks to email, that's an easy thing to do. In fact, one of email's most valuable traits is that it allows people to spread ideas around quickly and inexpensively. That's why so many companies use email as a work tool. It's also how we'll use email in this class, as a way to help you do your writing work . . . for now I want you to use email as your thinking tool. We'll begin this journal writing very simply. The only real rule is to concentrate on ideas. There are no rights or wrongs here, as long as everyone is polite. And don't worry about spelling or grammar. These won't be graded, so just do the best you can. . . . Here's how to get started. . . . Write another short statement telling the people about the project you are working on. . . . Finally, ask the people to write back to you with their ideas about the project. Ask them to tell you what interests them about the project. Also ask them for at least 3 specific ideas of things you could write about for the project or include on your web page. Be sure to have them explain these ideas so that you could use them if you wanted to. (1999, 109–10)

This journal assignment seemed to fit very well with the goals I had for my technical writing course. It was project-oriented, aimed at accomplishing real work, and very business-like in manner. I thought these journals would not only be useful technical writing tools for my students, but also valuable documents for their learning.

Yet even though I liked this new journal writing assignment, I still worried about it a little. I thought that perhaps I had made the assignment a bit too prescriptive, perhaps directed the students too much in what they were to write for their journal entries. Some of journal writing's appeal lies in the personal freedom of expression it allows a writer, and I was afraid I might be sabotaging that appeal by focusing all of my technical writing students' journaling efforts on their projects. Could journal writing be worthwhile if it didn't include personal explorations of experiences and events or idiosyncratic thoughts, musings, and ramblings?

I wasn't sure. But at least now I had a place to start. I had stressed in the assignment that "a journal is primarily a place to work with ideas." And my journal assignment offered a place not only to record those ideas, but also a way to share those ideas with others on a regular basis. These journals were a tool for sharing. True, that community building might come at the expense of some of a journal writer's personal freedom, but the trade-off seemed worthwhile to me. In fact, that trade-off seemed to make the journals much like any other technical writing document, a written text that involved a negotiation between writer and audience. In other words, journaling had at last found a home in my technical writing course.

Closing the Journal

By writing stories about work, both as a teacher and as a technical writer, I was able to rethink my pedagogy. I came to see that my reluctance to use journals in my technical writing courses was rooted in a limited vision of these tools. Once the story opened my eyes, I was able to reconceive the journal assignment, bringing it into line with some of my other experience-based beliefs about technical writing practice. New visions reveal new paths to travel. For me though, these new visions come from looking backward, to stories about the places I've already been and the things I've already done.

Of course, not every set of stories proves to be so enlightening. I've chosen a story here that works the way I want it to. And that's after searching and searching through stories that didn't work. I had to read a number of old journals before I hit on exactly what I wanted. But that wasn't such a bad thing. Reading those journal entries took me back, called to mind sharing stories with people at the office, goofing off playing video games when the boss wasn't around, reading and editing each others' work, winning a design award for the *Application Processing* manual (1989), working until 3 A.M. to get final copy to the printers. Those were good times.

I'm glad when stories can help improve my teaching. But I'm even gladder when stories can bring back my friends, even for a moment. Which, I suppose, is why I keep a journal. That, and for entries like this:

> Went to see Oliver Stone's new movie *The Doors*. It was great. Went straight out after that and bought the greatest hits CD. Geoff had gone to see it too, and we sat talking about it over lunch. Everybody else had gone for Chinese, but we were trying to get the IBM manual done, so we said we'd have a working lunch. But then Geoff started telling me about the time he saw The Doors in concert. So I dug out my CD and we played "Riders on the Storm" and listened to Jim Morrison singing, and the rain drops and the thunder claps, and I told Geoff all we needed was a couple of lighters to wave in the air, and we'd be at the concert. But he had closed his eyes and was nodding to the music, and I knew he was already there.

PART SIX

School Stories

I started graduate school by missing class. I was signed up to take a course called "Curriculum and Instruction 975: General Seminar on Current Research in Writing Instruction." It was the first graduate course I would ever take. I hadn't even been formally admitted to the graduate program yet.

When I got my college timetable for that semester, I opened it up and checked the room, 415 Teacher Education Building, and the time 2:30–6:00 P.M. T. I showed up the following Thursday and found the room door was locked. Not only was no one waiting in front of the room, I couldn't find anyone on the same floor.

I finally found one person in an office on the third floor. He was a tall, curly-haired guy wearing a black turtleneck. His office was stacked nearly to the ceiling with boxes, and he was looking at several piles of papers and hopelessly trying to sort all the stuff out.

"Hi," I said.

"Hello," he said.

"You wouldn't happen to have a timetable in all this, in here . . . ," I said, my voice trailing off.

He laughed and said, "As a matter of fact, that's the one thing I did manage to unpack." Then he opened up a desk drawer and fished out the book for me.

I flipped through the class listings, found C & I 975, and reread the listing, which still said, "2:30–6:00 P.M. T."

"Shit!" I said. Then I looked up and realized on top of everything else, I had just sworn in front of the department's newest faculty member.

"What?" he asked.

"Oh, I misread the stupid timetable. My class meets on Tuesday. 'T' is for Tuesday. They use 'R' for Thursday."

"I think they do that everywhere," he said.

"I know. That's the really annoying part. I've been to hundreds of classes before and I've never forgotten how to read the timetable. I guess I just spaced out or something. Typical. And so now I've already missed my first graduate class."

He leaned over the book to check for himself. "Which class?" he asked.

"975. Professor Kean, I believe."

"Oh, Jack Kean. He's a great guy. You're going to love having a class with him."

"Yeah, after I get done explaining what an idiot I am."

"That too," he said, and extended his hand. "I'm Dave. Dave Schaafsma."

"Pleased to meet you," I said. "I'm Gian."

We shook hands and smiled.

"So what do you teach?" I asked. "I mean, what are you going to teach, if you ever get all these boxes unpacked?"

Dave laughed. "Oh, they hired me to teach a class on narrative inquiry. I'm going to teach that next spring."

"Really?" I said. "What's narrative inquiry?"

Narrative inquiry, as it happened, turned out to be the focus of the dissertation I would eventually write, with David Schaafsma as my director. That also turned out to be the tidiest I would ever see Dave's office.

Graduate school can be funny that way.

———

I had this great little car while I was in graduate school. It was a white Toyota Tercel with a red-and-black sporty stripe down the sides. It was a bit boxy shaped, but the engine ran great, and I could do a U-turn in the Tercel on any street, no matter how small. I also could park in spaces that were too small for most other cars. Parking at the University of Wisconsin-Madison was at least forty bucks a month, so being able to find the occasional free spot was a real bonus.

Three years after meeting Dave Schaafsma, I was pulling my Tercel into the K-Mart on Mendotta Drive. I needed brake fluid, and there were still a lot of K-Marts around in those days.

I had the radio on, WMAD I think, and they had a Berkeley professor on talking about the Rodney King trial. The professor said there had been a "paradigm shift in the legal world that had led to the trial results."

"Perhaps you could explain the word 'paradigm' for our listeners, Professor McCoy? A lot of them may not be familiar with the term."

"Well, certainly," said the professor. "A paradigm shift occurs when our prior modes of data analysis lose their ability to explain new phenomena. We then need to develop new ideological schema to account for the new datum. The paradigm notion stems from Thomas Kuhn's seminal work."

"1962!" I shouted. "*The Structure of Scientific Revolutions.* That's crystalized it for them, Professor," I said. I switched stations, and "Go Back to Your Woods" from Robbie Robertson's *Storyville* album whooshed out of my speakers.

Still, that is an interesting notion, whether the legal system has actually shifted paradigms. Not a bad application of Kuhn, I thought.

"Oh, please," I said to Robbie, since no one else was there to hear me. "Do we really need all of this academic jargon?" And then, since the parking lot was pretty empty, I let the words tumble out of me like my own pop song:

paradigmatic
symptomatic
epistomologic

epistomologiCAL
dialogiCAL
sociohistorical
poststructural
ideological
eth-no-meth-o-do-log-i-cal

critical theory
critical pedagogy
hegemony
heteroglossia
onomatopoeia

That's right, I thought. *Nobody knows what any of these words means. We're speaking our own language, so we don't have to talk to any real people about how to solve the world's very real problems.*

And even if they had heard the words before, then we'd tell them that nothing actually means anything at all, all meaning is fluid, it shifts and changes until you're never sure where you are or who you are or what paradigm you're in or what ideology you're subscribing to.

Then I started thinking about all the people I couldn't seem to talk to anymore: my parents, my students, and my friends. Nobody seemed to understand the issues I was thinking about. Nobody talked like me. The only people on my page now were other graduate students. What good did it do to learn a language nobody seemed to speak?

I really need to get a life, I thought, not for the last time.

I'm in Kentucky and I'm presenting a professional paper on multicultural education at the prestigious National Council of Teachers of English Conference. But really it's just a story. I'm reading a kid's story about what education is like for him. "If you want to understand him, then listen to him," I think as I read.

But it's a goofy story too, a mix of science and gummi bears, and I wonder if Brandon were here whether anyone would listen to what he had to say. And then I start to wonder if anyone's actually listening to what I'm saying. Then I see somebody get up and walk out of the room, and I panic and lose my place in the paper and have to get my friend, Dawn, to remind me where I was at.

Afterwards, I say to Dawn, "Well, there's nowhere to go in academia but up after that disaster."

Years later, I'm standing at the tee box on hole #2 at the Chestnut Ridge Country Club. It's a nice, long gently sloping downhill shot, but it's narrow and the left trees are out of bounds. The air is still cool and there's a little fog, but the sun is working its way up. It'll be a perfect day for golf.

"Hey, Gian," says my golfing partner. "Yesterday, when I bumped into you on the street. You remember that guy who was talking about his new pedagogical approach?"

"Oh, Bill? Yeah, I remember. I think," I said.

"What does pedagogical mean?"

"It means. Well, basically it's just another word for teaching. That's all it means really. Pedagogy is just how you teach."

"Oh. So why do you call it pedagogy then?"

"We just like the word, Zach, old boy. We just like the word."

Another time, a friend of mine tells me how glad she will be to finish graduate school. "It's such a lonely business," she says. "We're isolated in this academic world. People don't talk to each other. One department never sees another. Two profs are never in the same class at once. Even when we read other people's papers, it's just to take pieces for our own work. All this research and reading and writing. It helps us learn, but what does it help us do? Theories open our eyes but what unties our hands?"

I don't know what to say to that, so I offer to buy her a Coke.

———

I'm teaching an introductory composition class in the summer, June 12th, and a few of us are talking about an article. But most of the students are just sitting there, maybe listening, mostly trying to stay cool. And then, right in front of me, right in the middle of the first row, Jennifer yawns. Loudly.

"Sorry," she says and blushes.

I stop mid-sentence, put down my book, look at the class, and say, "OK. That's the end of that. What do you think we should be doing in here? What would make this class actually worth being in?"

I wait, for a while, until somebody finally says, "Maybe we could, I don't know, write a story about something funny that happened to us?"

"Funny stories. OK. That's a start." I write "Funny Stories" on the board.

"What about politics? This year's the presidential election. Could we maybe read some political stories?"

"Boring," someone else says.

"Hey," I say, "We're just making a list of ideas." I write "Political Stories" on the board.

"I had this class one time," says Marc, from the back row. "We had to write our own obituary. It was actually pretty interesting."

"Not bad," I say. I write "Obituaries" on the board.

"How about working on our resumes?"

"What about writing letters to the campus paper?"

"I should write my mom," says a guy by the window.

"We could write to Santa Claus."

"Maybe we could try writing to the provost to see if we can get some new computers for this room," I say.

Before long, the board is full of ideas.

"Alright," I say. "Let's vote on the best three ideas and those are the ones we'll do."

"Why do we have to vote?" asks Adam. "Why can't we just do them all?"

"Well," I say. "We don't have all that much time."

"We've got plenty of time," he says. "We can start today."

———

Someone gets this great idea to hold a Young Writer's Conference at the Indiana Junior High, and I wind up trying to teach a room full of 13-year-olds how to write poetry. Naturally, I drag my wife into it.

We use my father's book, *Face the Poem,* and get the kids to write animal poems and then give them construction paper and scissors and markers and glue and string and tell them to make masks. Of course, the scissors are those safe school scissors with the rounded ends that won't cut anything, so we have to use our fingers to punch the eyeholes. But it works, pretty well.

"Is a dragon an animal?" a little boy asks me.

"Is a dragon an animal?" I repeat. "Yeah, I guess so."

"Can I make a dragon then?" he says, shaking a big green piece of construction paper up and down in his hands.

"It's awfully hard to make a dragon," I say. "They have all those spikes on their head."

"You could use red paper for the fire, Corey," says a girl at the next desk.

"Good idea," says Corey.

"Are you sure you want to make a dragon?" I ask Corey. "Do you think you can?"

"You bet. The best stories have dragons in them."

"That's true," I say. "Those are the best stories."

Extra Cookies

"You should sleep with your head to the east,"
Dad said, as he and Mom put sheets on the bed.
I was putting clothes in the dresser drawers
of my new dorm room.
"Why?" I asked.
"It's a spiritual thing," he said.

After unpacking everything,
we bought lunch at Kohl's Grocery store
and had a picnic.
We ate California pears,
thin slices of beef on hard rolls,
and Stella D'oro sponge cookies.
"You can keep the extra cookies," Mom said.
But then she forgot to give them to me,
so they stayed in a bag in the trunk.

After lunch, I watched them drive away;
Finally I was a college student.
The day had ten hours left,
Time to meet people
And start a life.
I stayed up late,
Stretching out the day for all it was worth.

But now the day is gone
And the only story I have kept
Is of the missing cookies.

Telling Stories with Students

Case sat in the loft with the dermatrodes strapped across his forehead, watching motes dance in the diluted sunlight that filtered through the grid overhead. A countdown was in progress in one corner of the monitor screen. . . .

The screen bleeped a two-second warning.

The new switch was patched into his Sendai with a thin ribbon of fiberoptics.

And one and two and—

Cyberspace slid into existence from the cardinal points. Smooth, he thought, but not smooth enough. Have to work on it. . . .

Then he keyed the new switch.

The abrupt jolt into other flesh. Matrix gone, a wave of sound and color. . . . She was moving through a crowded street, past stalls vending discount software, prices feltpenned on sheets of plastic, fragments of music from countless speakers. Smells of urine, free monomers, perfume, patties of frying krill. For a few frightened seconds he fought helplessly to control her body. Then he willed himself into passivity, became the passenger behind her eyes. (Gibson 1984, 55–56)

This quote comes from William Gibson's dark futuristic novel *Neuromancer*. It's a work of science fiction, more accurately a work of cyberpunk fiction, about a future time when people can plug their brains directly into computers in order to control them. *Neuromancer* tells the story of a washed-up computer hacker named Case who gets hired to hack into a computer with artificial intelligence. *Neuromancer* is a well-written story, and illuminating, especially in light of our ever-increasing dependence on computer systems. These days I'd even be inclined to call the book a classic.

Since I've already devoted so much of this book to talking about the need to value stories, all kinds of stories, I hope I don't have to confront any anti–science fiction biases. In particular, I've talked about the need to listen to our students' stories, which means if they want to write science fiction stories, we ought to let them do just that. This is certainly one of the fundamental beliefs of narrative ideology, that teachers should create opportunities for students to tell their own stories. Trousdale, Woestehoff, and Schwartz promote this in their book, *Give a Listen*:

> It is time we looked more closely at storytelling as an important and revitalizing component of our classroom environment. . . . Can older students learn more sophisticated language patterns through the telling of stories as well? We believe they can—and do. For older children, the oral sharing of stories breaks down walls of isolation, often becoming the glue that holds together a diverse set of community members, giving them a common language experience along with deeper understanding of one another. (1994, ix)

Trousdale, Woestehoff, and Schwartz are convinced that classroom storytelling, both written and oral, helps students develop into highly competent language users. In "Gilbert's and Dave's Stories: Narrative and Knowing," Schaafsma also talks about stories as a valuable learning tool for students: "We who teach often dismiss stories as a primitive form, a form for children, something students need to move 'beyond' for the learning they will have to do in schools. However, stories, grounded as they are in students' lives and concerns, are one important means students have for making sense of their worlds, an important tool for learning" (1989, 89). Finally, Pierce, Terry, and Ferguson, in "Storytelling: An Effective Tool for Promoting Literacy and Language Development," add even more claims to the list of benefits to be accrued by students who are encouraged to tell their stories: "Storytelling can build confidence and poise, develop a love of language and stories, stimulate critical thinking, develop appreciation of other ethnic cultures, build listening skills . . . and improve expressive and receptive skills" (1997, 67).

It seems clear that many teachers firmly believe in the benefits of asking students to tell stories. In line with these arguments, I could use this chapter to offer one or more students' storytelling efforts up for consideration. While that certainly could be useful, I wish, instead, to offer a slight twist on this storytelling process. Rather than offer just one student telling a story, I would like to discuss how a student and teacher *together* came to write a story. I believe in this way I can follow the above calls for student stories while also offering something new.

So allow me to draw attention back to my opening quote. This passage from *Neuromancer* describes the computerized bonding of two people's minds, something that is technologically possible in the future Gibson foresees. This is the key issue of interest for me in this story, the notion of actually linking two disparate personalities, creating "the abrupt jolt into other flesh." This idea is actually not that far in the future. Cybernetics professor Kevin Warwick (2000) has actually conducted experiments in which a computer monitored a small silicon chip that was surgically implanted into his arm for nine days. While Warwick couldn't use his mind to control the computer, the computer was able to monitor Warwick's physical location and do things like open doors as he approached them and turn on lights as he entered a room. Warwick plans to use the link to have the computer send nerve stimuli to his brain in a later experiment.

Now it might be asking a bit much to request that teachers allow their students to be hardwired into their heads. I do think, though, that there are ways in which people can link their minds through collaborative storytelling. In my doctoral thesis, "Cyberwriting: A Story of Teaching, Learning, and Co-authoring" (1995), I described a one-year study I conducted examining the collaborative writing done by a high school student and a writing teacher. My thesis detailed the slow, shifting process of change involved in moving from a teacher-student relationship to a coauthor relationship. While researchers such as Bruffee (1984) and Ede and Lunsford (1983) strongly advocate collaborative learning and collaborative writing, we have few pictures of how such collaboration looks. Building on the work of Bakhtin (1981), I would here like to discuss the potentialities of student-teacher collaborative story writing.

The Story Writers

Because coauthoring is a collaborative act, it is a process that is intimately connected to the specific people who take part in the collaboration. In fact, Ede and Lunsford point out that it is the differences between individual writers that often make the collaborative writing process difficult (1983, 151). But whereas Ede and Lunsford shy away from describing these idiosyncratic differences, my research suggests that these personal differences greatly affect the type of collaboration that is possible between writers. Thus to understand the collaborative story writing that this study describes, it is useful to know some details about the writers involved: In this case there were two of us, a high school student, whom I'll call Dustin, and myself, at the time a graduate student in an English education doctoral program.

Dustin

When I met Dustin he was already a lone wolf though he was only about four-teen years old. He usually wore army boots, khaki pants, punk rock T-shirts under unbuttoned flannel shirts, and sometimes a black leather biker's jacket. Dustin walked with an easy gait. On one side of his head his brown hair hung down over his eyes. He constantly had to brush it aside. The other half of his head was partly shaven. Dustin had been homeschooled on and off by his parents as he was growing up. He wrote horror stories and song lyrics and his parents had told me he liked to write. He didn't talk much, at least not to me.

Gian

I was in my late twenties at the time. I had graduated from the University of Wisconsin with an English and journalism double major. Then I had spent a few years writing computer manuals for a technical writing company. I mostly dressed in T-shirts and jeans, kept my hair cut short, but not shaved, and was a product of Wisconsin's public school system. I liked to write "seri-ous" fiction and watch movies. Dustin and I were quite different, and we both knew it.

The Story Writing Context

Dustin was homeschooled, which gave us freedom to do some kinds of writ-ing one can't do in many schools. In any case, I have used cowriting in my own classrooms, and I believe its benefits can be obtained in most schools. Though they homeschooled Dustin, his parents didn't know much about teaching writing, for which they had contacted a university outreach pro-gram. In such mentorships, a university graduate student usually works one-on-one with a high school student in a specific subject area.

The mentorship Dustin and I set up with the aid of his parents con-sisted of weekly meetings between the two of us in which we would discuss Dustin's writing. I would have total freedom to direct Dustin's writing instruction. His parents' job would be to make sure he kept up with weekly assignments.

The First Five Months of the Mentorship

When I started, I had few specific goals for teaching Dustin. He had told his parents that he wanted to become a writer, and my job was to help him work toward that goal. We decided to concentrate Dustin's work on creative writing. As a technical writer, I might have steered Dustin toward more professional types of writing, given that technical writing was a booming field at the time. But, as a veteran technical writer, I had to admit that writing computer manuals was a little dull. I figured that if Dustin wanted to become a real writer, he might as well work toward becoming a novelist, even if the odds were against that actually happening.

One of the real pleasures of homeschooling was that I was under no pressure to teach Dustin particular types of academic genres, such as an expository essay or a standard research report. Figuring he could always learn those things later, I decided instead to have Dustin work on writing stories. Another advantage of homeschooling was that Dustin was free to spend as much time as he wanted writing each day. He didn't have regular classes he had to attend. I thought this was a great opportunity for a budding young writer since with some hard work and dedication, he could have volumes of material written by the time he became an adult, easily paving the way for a possible future career as a fiction writer. I figured it was certainly within the realm of possibility, anyway.

As I saw it, there were two main things that were important to being a creative writer. One was learning to be a good reader of everything from books to movies to television commercials. The other was to write things that gave some insight on contemporary life, what is generally called realistic or serious fiction. This was the kind of writing I did. It was also the kind of writing that my favorite authors did, people like Tobias Wolff (1989) and Amy Tan (1989). Because Dustin was a young teenager, I thought he was in a good position to tell people what it was like to be a teenager in the 1990s. Adults write most teen fiction, so I thought Dustin could actually tell the real story of teenage life.

I spent five months pursuing these goals with Dustin, trying many techniques, like freewriting and brainstorming, that I had learned about in my composition theory graduate coursework. But I always let Dustin choose what he wanted to write about, and again and again he gave me stories of horror and fantasy. Dustin consistently refused to write anything I viewed as realistic. He wouldn't keep a journal. I could barely even get him to talk about his writing, mostly just "Yes," "No," or "I don't know." He never read any of the stories or watched any of the films that I suggested were related to his pieces of writing. He was content to stay writing in his fantasy genre and resisted all my efforts to move him out of it. In short, Dustin's own goals as a writer did not match my goals for him as his teacher.

Eventually this started to frustrate me. Like many English teachers, I wouldn't have minded discovering the next James Joyce, but my goals didn't include helping my students write novels like those of Stephen King (1988) or J. R. R. Tolkien (1965). *Where was the value in that?* I thought. As an English major in college, I had studied literature, and we certainly hadn't read any Stephen King. It never occurred to me, of course, that I might have had a rather biased view about literature.

I wasn't the only one getting frustrated with the work, either. It seemed to me that Dustin wasn't very happy with how our class sessions were going. He began to forget to bring his work to our meetings or to have some reason he hadn't found time to write during a particular week. What he did write got shorter and shorter and felt rushed when I read it. Sometimes he'd tell me that he had just written a piece the hour before we met. Neither Dustin's goals as a writer nor my goals as a teacher were being met. I began to wonder if I should just back out of the mentorship.

Coauthoring Stories

As the frustrations mounted and our first semester drew to a close, I decided it definitely was time to end the mentorship. But then, unexpectedly, a collection of events stopped me. The first event was an end-of-the-semester meeting with Dustin and his father. During the meeting Dustin said that he had really liked how I read his drafts carefully and cared about what he said. Given how the semester had gone, I was stunned to hear him make such a statement. I had never thought Dustin liked having me read his stuff at all. Half the time, I thought he viewed me as an intruder into the private world of his writing. But apparently, I had misread Dustin's reactions to having me read his work. He actually liked having someone that thought carefully about what he was saying. It was also at this time that a friend gave me the copy of William Gibson's *Neuromancer* with which I opened this chapter. Not only had I found the book fascinating, but by sheer coincidence, Dustin was also reading it. For a moment that day, at least, I wondered if maybe Dustin and I weren't that different after all.

I was convinced now that Dustin did value the mentorship. Also to my surprise, I had found that Dustin and I both shared a common interest: cyberpunk. Having found this common ground and having gained new energy for our working relationship, the two of us decided to write a cyberpunk story together. We planned to each write sections separately that would connect to a central character, a teenager living in a cyberpunk world. We planned eventually to link these sections together in a larger narrative.

We had no real guides or models at the time to help us figure out how to write together. In fact, Brodkey (1987) says it is hard to even envision writing as a social act because our societal images of writing are so often solitary, "a writer alone in a cold garret" (54). So Dustin and I didn't start out as equal writers on a joint project. For instance, early on, when I asked Dustin how many pages of the story he could write for the following week, he turned the question back at me and asked how much I thought he could write. Of course, in a strictly writer-writer relationship, presumably each writer would work at his own pace. But we were not cowriters yet; we were still teacher and student, and of course in most schools, it is the teachers, not the students, who decide how much the students are to write. As Stuart Greene (1993) has described, students often approach writing tasks based on their past experiences with school. Dustin expected me, as the teacher, to direct him, even though we were collaborating. He even left it up to me to pick what idea we would write about. I found I had to struggle to make our relationship more equal. Simply saying we were coauthors did not make it so.

And even as we tried to work out what a coauthorship was like, we continued to work as if we were still single authors. I kept a research journal about our work, and near the end of one entry, I made only a brief mention about trying to integrate the two stories: "Dustin starts suggesting ways to integrate our two stories into one larger story." Before then, most of our talk at best only compared our two pieces of writing rather than trying to fuse them together. We also made no plans to use each other's characters or plots. Instead we talked about the setting of our story. What year was it? What city did the characters live in? How much did food cost? Would there be street gangs in the future? How much would computers cost? This was neutral ground that we could agree upon without having to make major changes to our own individual story lines or characters.

As we finally began to combine all the pages of our writing into one story, we found we had to leave behind not only our roles of teacher and student, but also our roles as *individual* writers. Instead we at last became true coauthors.

In the end, Dustin and I were able to work together on a way to fuse our two separate stories into one complete story. We did this by playing with the idea of the individual consciousness. In the next section, I've included a short story about how one of our last days writing together turned out.

Two Become One

We started to play with the idea of blending our stories together. What if we tried for chaos instead of coherence? What if we left things unfinished? Had one story line kind of melt into another? Say Dustin's main character, Duke, gets on a subway, but Gian's character, Quill, gets off, and then some other character, like Eagle, gets back on. And all the time the reader would be asking, What happened to those other characters?

Then Dustin asked, "What if we used first person, but the *I* would represent different people all at once? Like: 'I walked up to the bank window, and pulled out a gun. I saw the man point a gun at me, so I gave him money from the cash register.' We could have multiple *I*s.

"The real story would be a person who . . . didn't know who he was anymore. He wouldn't have his own *I* at all; he'd be constantly jumping around since everything was really just happening in his own mind."

"Not bad," I said. "I think I can see how that would work. And that way, we can keep whatever we want from everything we've both written. This is great."

In the end our story focused on how in the cyberpunk world of computer-generated reality, a person was no longer a single *I*. And, as it turned out, this was the same thing Dustin and I—*we*—had learned by writing together in the real world, that we couldn't hold onto our individual *I*s in cowriting a story because there couldn't be just one author. We had finally learned to see language the way Bakhtin describes it, "the word in language is half someone else's" (1981, 293).

The Benefits of Coauthoring Stories

Over the course of my collaborative story writing with Dustin, I observed many benefits that came from this teacher-student coauthoring. The most obvious was the student's motivation to write. Shortly after the cowriting began, I noted in my research journal that Dustin wrote "a record 8 pages." During the first semester, I felt lucky to get Dustin to write even one page for me. Teacher motivation, though, is just as important as student motivation, so it is significant that the story coauthoring also led me to write this entry in my research journal: "I'm happy about the overall direction things are taking. . . . The story and Dustin's writing has potential. Dustin's talking a lot, and I'm having a good time. I'm looking forward to the sessions now, not dreading them the way I had last semester."

Our joint writing endeavor also allowed for new kinds of talk to happen between teacher and student. In another journal entry, I wrote, "We start class by exchanging papers. Dustin says I have a lot of descriptions in mine. Something he admits to kind of having forgotten to write. He says he'll work on that." At this point in the year, we were finally beginning to talk as if we were two writers trying to help each other rather than just a teacher trying to evaluate a student's work. I could easily have told Dustin his story needed some descriptions to add clarity, but because our stories were part of a joint effort, Dustin immediately saw a connection between his writing and my own. He could imagine how my method of writing could work in his own piece because the two pieces shared the same context. Teachers often assume that students learn to write better when they are given models of good writing, but without also creating a context in which students can use those models, the models themselves often fail to be of any help to students. In this case, Dustin could instantly see the connection between my modeling and his own writing because of our shared story writing context.

Dustin made other breakthroughs as well because of the collaborative writing. In another journal entry, I wrote:

> We talk about virtual reality [computer simulations of reality]. Dustin's seen a version of it in the new Stephen King film *The Lawnmower Man* [Leonard 1992]. He says it was good, though not a real cyberpunk movie as we had thought it might be. He tells me how he's been discussing [our] story with one of his friends and how that discussion led to a section in the piece he wrote. He also considered looking up the name of a body part he described.

As I have said, early on I constantly referred Dustin to outside sources that related to what he was writing. Yet I never achieved my goal of making him see how this reading might connect to his writing. Now, though, he was suddenly seeing this link on his own, perhaps partly because he was imitating a way of thinking about writing that I had modeled for him, but probably mostly because he was much more invested in working with me on this project and had seen how I thought about writing. As I observed in my research journal, "I'm stunned by all this sudden intertextuality."

Finally Living the Narrative Life

Dustin was not the only one who made breakthroughs in this collaborative story writing process either. As I tried to write my parts of the cyberpunk story, I found I had to consider what things would make a cyberpunk story interesting to me. I had to ask what life would be like if you could plug your mind into a computer. What in this cyberpunk world would be like my own world? What would be different? What forms would politics, economics, and education take in such a world? What would people's relationships be like? What problems and ethical issues would people struggle with? I found myself awakening to the power of the story on which Dustin and I were collaborating. It was a good story, and its nuances began to pull me in, even forcing me to move beyond my biases about what great literature was. I began to see how this story, like any story, allowed me an infinite number of ways to explore and think about the world in which I was living, to make meaning out of that world.

As I worked on my sections of the story, I also began to see why Dustin was so interested in cyberpunk and why he was always writing stories about horror and fantasy and alternate world experiences. For one thing, in a world where computers could create personal realities for people, it was easy to be a loner. This would appeal to a loner like Dustin. There was a lot of rebellion in the cyberpunk world, too, with which Dustin could also identify. Most importantly, perhaps, in a world where power is linked to computers, teenagers can take control of their own destinies. In *Neuromancer,* a group of teenage terrorists, called the Panther Moderns, are as influential as the businessmen and military leaders whose paths they cross. It was no wonder Dustin would want to write about cyberpunk, because in that world, young teenagers could do almost whatever they wanted. By writing about this world myself, I slowly came to understand not only what attracted Dustin to it, but also how asking Dustin to write about his life in the real world had been, in a way, asking him to accept the subservient role that society normally gives to teenagers. Why would a teen want to write "serious" fiction about teenage life, when that life was full of bossy authority figures, restricted movie ratings, and curfews? Once I understood that perhaps Dustin wanted to write stories that would provide him a way to escape some of the unpleasant realities of teenage life, I finally figured out why the teenage hero in Dustin's part of our story happened to be named Duke.

In fact, with each page I wrote of this cyberpunk story, the more I began to see it was a story Dustin and I had to tell. I began to see that as a teacher it really was valuable to write stories, especially stories that students cared about. Not only that, but I came to understand and believe that the story had value for me as well as for Dustin. Once I started valuing the stories that Dustin thought were valuable, I was finally able to figure out what literacy meant for him. Dustin needed a literacy that would help him explore and understand his world, the mixed-up world of being a teenager, the sort of literacy Dyson (1991) has described. For Dustin, this turned out to be a literacy of fantasy and science fiction stories. When I quit pushing Dustin away from the literacy stories he valued and tried instead to find my own meaning in the stories he was drawn to, Dustin finally responded to my teaching.

I think by writing with Dustin, I started to become the kind of genuine listener that Schuster (1990) has said teachers need to be. As I wrote with Dustin, I slowly learned to hear the stories he was trying to tell me. As long as I was reading Dustin's writing like a teacher, so I could evaluate it or find a way to make it match the kind of writing I liked, I could hold onto the stories I valued. But when I started writing with Dustin, I found I had committed myself to also valuing Dustin's stories. I had linked my mind to his, forced myself to experience "the abrupt jolt into other flesh."

Of course, there is one other benefit to coauthoring stories that cannot be overlooked. As I wrote at the end of my March 5th research journal entry, "I leave feeling good and Dustin seems actually a little excited or enthusiastic for once." When we leave behind our roles of teachers and students in order to become co-storytellers, education becomes not only meaningful, but enjoyable. If we can do this, then we have truly begun to live the narrative life.

Travelers' Tales

Cormac sits on the roof of my car and points. A semi-truck roars pasts and blasts its horn. Cormac shouts and laughs. I pick him up and carry him, with his bottle, toward the freeway rest stop. We are on a road trip. It is the 20th of May and we have just crossed the Ohio border. We are on our way to see Cormac's grandparents in Wisconsin, 720 miles of flat highways, McDonald's restaurants, and farmland.

"This will be a good story," I tell Cormac.

He looks at me, then stretches out a small hand, reaching for my glasses.

"Hey! You're missing the point." I laugh and hold him up above my head and he smiles and giggles.

"The story of our road trip," I tell him again. "Just you and me on the open road."

We buy corn chowder in a bread bowl from a Panera Bread restaurant and milk and juice and a container of orange Jell-O. I struggle to carry Cormac, his diaper bag, and the tray with the food and finally make it to a little table by a window, where I plop down our stuff. Then I look around for a high chair, finally spot a clean one, and fight Cormac as he kicks his legs while I'm getting him into the chair. He starts chewing a piece of sourdough bread; like all Italians, he loves to eat bread.

Then I sit down and start on the soup, but it is spicy and when I give a spoon to Cormac, he spits it back at me. I dig into the bag and find some green grapes which he prefers.

An older couple sit down at a table next to us and eat their lunch while I try to coax Cormac into eating more bread. He does, and I even get him to eat a few pieces dipped into the soup before he decides to start tossing things on the floor again.

"Would he eat a piece of banana?" the woman who was behind me asks.

146

I turn and see her husband carrying a tray off to one side. She is wearing a white and gold-flecked sweater with a blue broach on it.

"Sure," I say. "Bananas are his favorite."

"Take as much as you want," she says and holds the banana out to me.

I break off a third of the banana, split that in half, and hold it out to Cormac.

"Mmmmmmmm," he hums. He grabs the banana and mashes it down onto the table.

"Eat it," I say. I hold the banana to his mouth, and he tastes it and then grabs it from me to hold in his hand again. He squeezes the banana piece, but gets some into his other hand and pulls it up to his mouth.

"How old his he?" asks the woman.

"Just nine months. He's a good eater. He loves fruit."

We watch Cormac chew on the banana.

"We're driving out to see my parents," I say. "In Wisconsin. But it's taking us a while. I have to stop a lot to give him breaks."

"Where's his mother?" she asks.

"She's teaching back in Pennsylvania. They had to make up some snow days, so they won't be done for a few more weeks. But I have vacation now. So I decided to see how the trip would work out."

"Good for you," she says. "I bet his grandparents will love seeing him."

"Oh, yes," I say. "They can't wait."

"Too bad he's too little to remember the trip," she says.

"I'll just tell him about it," I say.

——————

Later, in the car, dusk sets in and I turn up the heat and steal a peek at Cormac asleep in the back. I have a yellow blanket wrapped around him and he chews on a corner of it, one tiny fist still clutching a plastic straw from the rest stop.

I put on a little music, Marc Cohn's *Burning the Daze* album (1998), and watch the road and the cars whizzing past. I am tired, and there are many miles to go still. I am wondering how Edel is doing, but there was no answer when I tried to phone earlier.

"You're very brave to try a trip like that, without Edel."

"He'll miss his mother."

"Maybe you ought to fly."

"What if he doesn't sleep? What if he cries?"

The skeptics of our journey were many. The dawn of the twenty-first century has not brought men too far into the world of childbearing. People enjoy thinking of fathers as helpless around babies. And Cormac does fidget in his sleep, like he's looking for her.

I try the phone again, but the answering machine clicks in and I figure she's still busy at school grading papers.

I try to stretch my back a little. The car is too small for me, but the mileage is good. I put on new tires before leaving. Another hour or two and I'll stop to get a hotel room, or I'll try to push through Chicago to reach my grandmother's house. If Cormac sleeps.

Still, it *is* a good story. Daddy and the baby on a road trip. Lewis and Clark breaking trail through the wilderness. I try not to think about the 15 hours going back.

———

Everyone talks about kids changing your life: the lack of sleep, the worry, the excitement, the laughs, the diapers, and the clothes shopping. It's all true, of course.

But I had forgotten all the stories. *Curious George, Make Way for Ducklings, Where the Wild Things Are, The 500 Hats of Bartholomew Cubbins, Tikki Tikki Tembo, Swimmy,* and on and on.[1] "Let the wild rumpus start."[2]

One day after Cormac was born I started making lists of all the old stories I could remember and went to Borders to look for the books, but the children's department was gigantic, full of tables and chairs, toys, kids, and shelf after shelf of books. I couldn't remember the authors, couldn't remember many of the titles. I just remembered the stories: talking animals, silly hats, rhymes, kids misbehaving, giants and wizards and witches and castles, and bright colors with crooked houses and spiraling staircases and stars and smiles.

So I called my mother. And got some of the book titles from her. And I went to the library, down the stairs to the children's section, and a nice woman knew the books I was talking about.

"Oh, yes, that's a great story," she kept saying. "Yes, yes, you'll have to read him that one."

Of course Cormac mostly chews on the books or slaps at them with his hands. He's too little to read stories to now. So all I can do is to plan for him, all the good stories we can share together. The children's books and then *The*

---

1. In the order they are listed, these wonderful children's books are by H. A. Rey (1969), Robert McCloskey (1969), Maurice Sendak (1963), Dr. Seuss (1966), Arlene Mosel (1968), and Leo Lionni (1963).
2. Quoted from *Where the Wild Things Are,* by Maurice Sendak.

Call of the Wild and *Tom Sawyer* and *Harry Potter and the Sorcerer's Stone.*[3]
And then, all the great movies, like *Star Wars* and *The Godfather* and *Thelma and Louise* and *Shrek.*[4] He has a whole world of stories just waiting for him, every one new and exciting and undiscovered.

But he's still too little for stories right now. He just wants to be held.

Maybe you're asking: "Why is he telling us this story? Why do we care about his son and their car trip and a bunch of children's fairy tales?"

It's a little overindulgent, isn't it? A typical new parent, wrapped up in the world of his child, boring everyone else with little stories of smiles and one-word sentences and faltering steps. Save it for the grandparents.

What does it really matter? What difference does any of this make?

And, of course, you're right.

But that's because these are my stories. They mostly matter to me, my son, my wife, and my family. Just the way your stories matter to you. But these stories, like all stories, count for everything. Without them, we're just molecules taking up space. We've got to tell our stories, no matter how small they are. It's the only thing we can do.

I've already said this, in the other chapters. Said it over and over in as many ways as I could think of. Talked about the need to tell stories of work and teaching and your family and your students and, of course, yourself. I've talked about teaching yourself to find the value in stories and to resist the antinarrative forces around you. I've tried to explore the ideological nature of narrative and to ground this explanation in a series of essays and poems and stories.

In the end, though, it all boils down to one simple argument. Stories matter.

Maybe that was all I needed to say?

So take that as the message. Put stories at the center. Start with small narratives, build to bigger narratives, use narratives to find your way. Don't cast stories aside. Don't teach your students that they have to leave their stories aside. Instead, celebrate the stories we have. Make the most of them.

Live for stories. Learn to live a narrative life.

---

3. These seminal books, in the order listed, are by Jack London (1903), Mark Twain (1961), and J. K. Rowling (1997).

4. The directors of these film classics, in the order listed, are George Lucas (1977), Francis Ford Coppola (1972), Ridley Scott (1991), and Vicky Jenson, Andrew Adamson, and Scott Marshall (2001).

Imagine a world where we pause, as the day passes, to hear more stories: the old man on the park bench, the woman filling your shopping bag, the person delivering your mail, yes, even the parent babbling about his beautiful baby. Read the stories in the newspaper. Smile at the clever stories of our politicians. Laugh at a story on television. Read a book in bed.

Tell someone the story of how you fell in love.

In the rush and hurry of life, in our overworked, stressed-out, multitasked, too many bills and too little cash, no time to eat, no time to wait, when will it be the weekend again world, we forget to take time for stories. Stories give us time to pause, to think, to breath. Stories keep us alive. Or at least, they can, if we will let them.

You want to make the world a better place? Tell somebody a good story.

Or make the most of a bad one. When the car jammed with most everything you own in the world overheats halfway from Sheboygan to your new apartment and stops dead in its track, remember, it'll be a good story. Like how you hiked two miles to get to a phone and when you got a lift back to your dead car, the cop was just about to slap one of those orange stickers on the windshield. But you got there at that precise moment and told her about the overheated engine, and just before she went to put the sticker away, you asked her if you could keep it, since you'd never actually gotten a chance to read one of those stickers and it would make a crazy kind of a souvenir.

We ought to spend more time collecting good stories for ourselves. We ought to spend more time telling good stories to each other. We ought to spend more of our lives *taking part* in good stories. And you know *exactly* the kind of story I mean, where people help each other out and say nice things to each other and do what's right and honest and fair and just. We *could* live in that kind of story world. If we wanted to. But we'd all have to set out to tell the right kind of stories.

The trouble is, stories with happy endings. Well, those are for kids' books. And most of us put those stories away, a long, long time ago.

I flip open the small silver phone and watch its face glow a luminescent blue. The phone gives off a small chime. I touch a few keys and phone home. Edel picks up.

"How's it going?" she asks.

"Pretty well. We stop every three or four hours because he likes to stretch his legs."

"He can't walk yet," Edel says and laughs.

"How are you doing?"

Edel launches into a story about some tessellation projects her math students are working on. She's trying to pack everything in as the year comes to a close. She teaches middle school students, and they're worried about a final exam they have to take in her class.

"But they'll do fine," she says.

"It's too bad you couldn't come along," I say. "But it's only a long weekend, really."

"I know," she says. "I love road trips."

"Well it's taking a lot longer than it usually does. We just can't seem to move as fast. I drive as far as I can without stopping while he's asleep, but that only lasts for about three hours or so."

"I just read a great story in *The New Yorker* about traveling."

"Really?" I say. "What's it called?"

"'Everything You Love Will Be Carried Away.'"

"That's a pretty depressing title."

"I know," Edel says. "It's by Stephen King. But it's really amazing."

"Read me a little."

"Ok," says Edel. "'To write a book like that, he thought you'd have to begin by talking about how it was to measure distance in green mile markers, and the very width of the land, and how the wind sounded when you got out of your car at one of those rest areas in Oklahoma or North Dakota. How it sounded almost like words.'"[5]

"Wow," I say.

"The guy's name is Alfie," Edel tells me. "He wants to write a book about bathroom graffiti."

"Graffiti?" I say.

"Yep. He's a traveling salesman. He copies graffiti phrases down from rest stops as he travels along the highway."

"Hunh," I say.

"Bet you never thought of collecting *those kinds* of stories," Edel says.

"You're right," I say. "Hmmm. I'll have to see if I can come up with anything good before I leave this stop."

Edel laughs. "See yah!" she says.

"We miss you," I say.

I flip the phone closed with a snap, and the blue light fades away.

---

5. Quoted from Stephen King's "Everything You Love Will Be Carried Away" in *The New Yorker*, 2001, p. 80.

Somewhere in the middle of Chicago, Cormac wakes in the backseat and starts to cry. I dig around on the seat beside me and eventually find some chocolate chip cookies and reach back with one. I feel his fingers wrap around the cookie, and he stops whimpering.

"It's ok," I tell him. "We'll be there soon."

He makes a few isolated cries, but he is eating now and kicking his feet against his car seat. I hand back two more cookies.

Outside, car lights streak past me at eighty miles an hour. Even at 1 A.M. the Chicago traffic is intense, careening through the night across five lanes of concrete. We drive past office buildings and billboards and shopping centers. Sometimes we see the Chicago L-train shooting past, sparks flying from its metal wheels, rolling toward the next stop and the tired workers trying to get home after another long day.

Inside the car, it grows quiet. Cormac drinks from a bottle of milk I've handed to him. He's getting sleepy again.

"That's a good boy," I say, softly. "Drink your milk. We're almost to grandma's house. It's not far now."

Cormac doesn't say anything.

"Tell you what," I say. "Maybe I can think of a good story. Sure. It goes something like this. Once upon a time. That's how all the good stories start."

Bibliography

Abt-Perkins, D., and G. S. Pagnucci, 1993. "From Tourist to Storyteller: Reading and Writing Science." In *The Astonishing Curriculum: Integrating Science and Humanities Through Language*, edited by Stephen Tchudi, 99–111. Urbana, IL: National Council of Teachers of English.

Akinnaso, F. Niyi. 2001. "Literacy and Individual Consciousness." In *Litearcy: A Critical Sourcebook*, edited by Ellen Cushman, Eugene R. Kintgen, Barry M. Kroll, and Mike Rose, 138–55. Boston: Bedford/St. Martin's.

Ancestry.com. 2003. Starter Collection. Accessed 1 September 2003 at *www.ancestry.com*.

Avildsen, John G. 1976. *Rocky.* Century City, CA: Metro-Goldwyn-Mayer Studios.

Bakhtin, Mikhail M. 1981. *The Dialogic Imagination.* Austin: University of Texas Press.

Barone, Thomas. 1992. "A Narrative of Enhanced Professionalism: Educational Researchers and Popular Storybooks About Schoolpeople." *Educational Researcher* 21 (8): 15–24.

Bartholomae, David. 1985. "Inventing the University." In *When a Writer Can't Write*, edited by Mike Rose, 134–65. New York: Guilford.

Behar, Ruth. 1996. *The Vulnerable Observer: Anthropology That Breaks Your Heart.* Boston: Beacon Press.

Blitz, Michael, and C. Mark Hurlbert. 1998. *Letters for the Living: Teaching Writing in a Violent Age.* Urbana, IL: National Council of Teachers of English.

BoDeans. 1991. *Black and White.* Los Angeles: Slash Records.

Brodkey, Linda. 1987. *Academic Writing as Social Practice*. Philadelphia: Temple University Press.

Bruffee, Kenneth A. 1984. Collaborative Learning and the Conversation of Mankind. *College English* 46: 635–52.

Bruner, Jerome. 1986. *Actual Minds, Possible Worlds*. Cambridge, MA: Harvard University Press.

———. 1990. *Acts of Meaning*. Cambridge, MA: Harvard University Press.

Carter, Kathy. 1993. "The Place of Story in the Study of Teaching and Teacher Education." *Educational Researcher* 22 (1): 5–12, 18.

Carver, Raymond. 1982. *What We Talk About When We Talk About Love*. New York: Vintage.

——— 1989. "Cathedral." In *Cathedral*, written by Raymond Carver, 209–28. New York: Vintage.

Cazden, Courtney, and Dell Hymes. 1978. "Narrative Thinking and Story-Telling Rights: A Folklorist's Clue to a Critique of Education." *Keystone Folklore* 22 (1–2): 22–35.

Ciardi, John. 1959. *Thirty-Nine Poems*. Piscataway, NJ: Rutgers University Press.

Ciulla, Joanne B. 2000. *The Working Life: The Promise and Betrayal of Modern Work*. New York: Three Rivers.

Clandinin, D. Jean, and F. Michael Connelley. 1995. *Teachers' Professional Knowledge Landscapes*. New York: Teachers College Press.

———. 1999. *Narrative Inquiry: Experience and Story in Qualitative Research*. San Francisco: Jossey-Bass.

Clapton, Eric. 1992. "Tears in Heaven." *Unplugged*. Burbank, CA: Reprise Records.

Clifford, John, ed. 1991. *The Experience of Reading: Louise Rosenblatt and Reader-Response Theory*. Portsmouth, NH: Boynton/Cook.

Cohan, Steven, and Linda M. Shires. 1988. *Telling Stories: A Theoretical Analysis of Narrative Fiction*. New York: Routledge.

Cohn, Marc. 1998. *Burning the Daze*. New York: Atlantic Recording Corporation.

Coles, Robert. 1989. *The Call of Stories. Teaching and the Moral Imagination.* Boston: Houghton Mifflin.

Connelly, F. Michael, and D. Jean Clandinin. 1990. "Stories of Experience and Narrative Inquiry." *Educational Researcher* 19 (5): 2–14.

Coppola, Francis Ford. 1972. *The Godfather.* Hollywood, CA: Paramount Studios.

Coupland, Douglas. 1994. *Life After God.* New York: Pocket.

Dhunpath, Rubby. 2000. "Life History Methodology: 'Narradigm' Regained." *International Journal of Qualitative Studies in Education* 13 (5): 543–51.

Diamant, Anita. 1997. *The Red Tent.* New York: St. Martin's Press.

Dillard, Annie. 1989. *The Writing Life.* New York: Harper and Row.

Doors, The. 1985. "Riders on the Storm." *Best of the Doors.* New York: Warner Music Group.

Doyle, Roddy. 1993. *Paddy Clarke Ha Ha Ha.* New York: Penguin.

Duncan, David James. 1995. *River Teeth: Stories and Writings.* New York: Doubleday.

Dyson, Anne H. 1991. "Viewpoints: The Word and the World—Reconceptualizing Written Language Development or Do Rainbows Mean a Lot to Little Girls?" *Research in the Teaching of English* 25 (1): 97–123.

Eagleton, Terry. 1991. *Ideology: An Introduction.* London: Verso.

Ede, Lisa, and Andrea A. Lunsford. 1983. "Why Write . . . Together?" *Rhetoric Review* 1: 150–57.

Egan, Kieran. 1979. *Educational Development.* New York: Oxford University Press.

————. 1986. *Teaching as Story Telling.* Chicago: University of Chicago Press.

Flower, Linda S. 1979. "Writer-Based Prose: A Cognitive Basis for Problems in Writing." *College English* 41: 19–37.

Fox, Gardner. (1968, September) "Tomorrow Kills the Justice League—Today!" In *The Justice League of America,* art by Dick Dillin and Sid Greene, (65): 1–22.

Franzen, Jonathan. 2001. *The Corrections (The Oprah Edition)*. New York: Farrar, Straus and Giroux.

———. 2003. *How to Be Alone: Essays*. New York: Farrar, Straus and Giroux.

Freedman, Susan G. 1990. *Small Victories: The Real World of a Teacher, Her Students, and Their High School*. New York: Harper and Row.

Freire, Paulo, and Donaldo Macedo. 1987. *Literacy: Reading the Word and the World*. South Hadley, MA: Bergin and Garvey.

Gannett, Cinthia. 1999. "Foreword: Two or Three Things I Know for Sure." In *The Personal Narrative: Writing Ourselves as Teachers and Scholars*, edited by Gil Haroian-Guerin, ix–xxii. Portland, ME: Calendar Island.

Gee, James Paul. 2001. "Literacy, Discourse, and Linguistics: *Introduction* and *What Is Literacy?*" In *Litearcy: A Critical Sourcebook*, edited by Ellen Cushman, Eugene R. Kintgen, Barry M. Kroll, and Mike Rose, 525–44. Boston: Bedford/St. Martin's.

Gibson, William. 1984. *Neuromancer*. New York: Ace.

Gillett, Margaret, and Ann Beer, eds. 1995. *Our Own Agendas: Autobiographical Essays by Women*. Montreal: McGill-Queen's University Press.

Gopnik, Adam. 2001. "The Story of Us All." *The New Yorker* (April): 37–38.

Goswami, Dixie, and Peter Stillman, eds. 1987. *Reclaiming the Classroom: Teacher Research as an Agent of Change*. Portsmouth, NH: Heinemann.

Green, Ann E. 1999. "The Places We Come From, the Places We're Going: Class, Race, and Writing." In *The Personal Narrative: Writing Ourselves as Teachers and Scholars*, edited by Gil Haroian-Guerin, 17–29. Portland, ME: Calendar Island.

Greene, Stuart. 1993. "The Role of Task in the Development of Academic Thinking Through Reading and Writing in a College History Course." *Research in the Teaching of English* 27 (1): 46–75.

Hampl, Patricia. 2000. "First Person Singular." In *One Blood: The Narrative Impulse*. Anchorage, AK: Alaska Quarterly Review.

Haroian-Guerin, Gil. 1999. "'The Slaughter of the Infants': Writing Ourselves into the New World." In *The Personal Narrative: Writing Ourselves as Teachers and Scholars*, edited by Gil Haroian-Guerin, 3–16. Portland, ME: Calendar Island.

Haswell, Richard, and Min-Zhan Lu. 2000. *Comp Tales*. New York: Longman.

Heath, Shirley Brice. 1983. *Ways with Words: Language, Life, and Work in Communities and Classrooms*. New York: Cambridge University Press.

Hemingway, Ernest. 1966. *The Short Stories*. New York: Collier.

Henry, Jeanne. 1995. *If Not Now: Developmental Readers in the College Classroom*. Portsmouth, NH : Boynton/Cook.

Hindman, Jane E. 2001. "Special Focus: Personal Writing: Introduction." *College English* 64 (1): 34–40.

———. 2003. "Special Issue: The Personal in Academic Writing." *College English* 66 (1): 9–20.

Hirsch Jr., Eric Donald. 1987. *Cultural Literacy: What Every American Needs to Know*. Boston: Houghton Mifflin.

Holquist, Michael. 1990. *Dialogism: Bakhtin and His World*. New York: Routledge.

Jenson, Vicky, Andrew Adamson, and Scott Marshall. 2001. *Shrek*. Hollywood, CA: Universal Studios.

Joyce, James. 1961. *Ulysses*. New York: Vintage Books.

King, Stephen. 1988. *The Gunslinger: The Dark Tower I*. New York: Plume.

———. 2000. *On Writing: A Memoir of the Craft*. New York: Scribner.

———. 2001. "Everything You Love Will Be Carried Away." *The New Yorker* (Jan.) 29: 74–80.

Kohl, Herb. 1988. *Thirty-Six Children*. New York: Plume.

Kuhn, Thomas. 1962. *The Structure of Scientific Revolutions*. Chicago: University of Chicago Press.

Kundera, Milan. 1986. *The Book of Laughter and Forgetting*. New York: Penguin.

———. 1988. *The Art of the Novel*. New York: Harper and Row.

Lawson, Mary. 2002. *Crow Lake*. New York: Delta Trade Paperbacks.

Lee, Stan. 1963. "Captain America Joins the Avengers." *The Avengers*. New York: Marvel Comics.

Lehmann, Chris. 2001 (December). "Literati: The Oprah Wars." *The American Prospect.* Accessed 1 July 2003 at *www.prospect.org/print/V12/21/lehmann-c.html.*

Leonard, Brett. 1992. *The Lawnmower Man.* New York: Warner.

Lionni, Leo. 1973. *Swimmy.* New York: Pinwheel.

London, Jack. 1903. *The Call of the Wild.* New York: Grosset & Dunlap.

Lucas, George. 1977. *Star Wars.* Los Angeles, CA: 20th Century Fox.

Macchio, Ralph. 2000. *X-Men Movie Adaptation.* New York: Marvel Comics.

Mackall, Joe. 1996. "Porch Stories: A Narrative Look at the Stories and the Storytelling Traditions of the Places My Students and I Call Home." Doctoral dissertation. Indiana, PA: Indiana University of Pennsylvania.

Martel, Yann. 2001. *Life of Pi.* New York: Harcourt.

Matejka, Ladislav, and I. R. Titunik. 1973. "Translator's Preface, 1986." In *Marxism and the Philosophy of Language,* written by V. N. Volosinov, translated by Ladislav Matejka and I. R. Titunik, vii–xii. Cambridge, MA: Harvard University Press.

Mayberry, Bob. 1999. "A Runaway Pancake and Tom Sawyer: Pleasures of Teaching the Text." In *The Personal Narrative: Writing Ourselves as Teachers and Scholars,* edited by Gil Haroian-Guerin, 116–26. Portland, ME: Calendar Island.

McCammon, Robert R. 1991. *Boy's Life.* New York: Pocket.

McCloskey, Robert. 1969. *Make Way for Ducklings.* New York: The Viking Press.

McEwan, Ian. 2001. *Atonement.* New York: Anchor Books.

Melville, Herman. 1964. *Moby-Dick.* Indianapolis: Bobbs-Merrill Company, Inc.

Meyer, Richard J. 1996. *Stories from the Heart: Teachers and Students Researching Their Literacy Lives.* Mahwah, NJ: Lawrence Erlbaum.

Miller, Janet L. 1990. *Creating Spaces and Finding Voices: Teachers Collaborating for Empowerment.* New York: State University of New York Press.

Mishler, Elliot G. 1986. *Research Interviewing: Context and Narrative.* Cambridge, MA: Harvard University Press.

Mitchell, Margaret. 1936. *Gone with the Wind.* New York: Macmillan.

Moore, Michael. 2002. *Stupid White Men . . . and Other Sorry Excuses for the State of the Nation.* New York: Regan/Harper Collins.

Morrison, Jim. 1985. *The Best of the Doors.* Los Angeles: Elektra/Asylum Records.

Morton, Kathryn. 1986. "The Storytelling Animal." *The Writer* 99 (Jan.): 3–4.

Mosel, Arlene. 1968. *Tikki Tikki Tembo.* New York: Scholastic.

Murray, Donald M. 1991. "All Writing Is Autobiography." *College Composition and Communication* 42 (1): 66–74.

————. 2002. *Write to Learn.* 7th ed. Philadelphia: Harcourt College.

Next Step Program, The. 2002. Next Step Program Overview. Accessed 1 May 2003 at *www.english.iup.edu/projects/nextstep/default.htm.*

O'Brien, Tim. 1990a. "How to Tell a True War Story." *The Things They Carried.* New York: Penguin. 73–92.

————. 1990b. "The Lives of the Dead." *The Things They Carried.* New York: Penguin. 253–73.

————. 1990c. "Notes." *The Things They Carried.* New York: Penguin. 175–82.

————. 1990d. *The Things They Carried.* New York: Penguin.

————. 1990e. "Sweetheart of the Song Tra Bong." In *The Things They Carried,* by Tim O'Brien, 99-125. New York: Penguin.

————. 1995. *In the Lake of the Woods.* New York: Penguin.

O'Connor, Joseph. 1994. *The Secret World of the Irish Male.* Dublin: New Island.

Ohmann, Richard. 1976. *English in America: A Radical View of the Profession.* New York: Oxford University Press.

Ong, Walter J. 2001. "Writing Is a Technology That Restructures Thought." In *Litearcy: A Critical Sourcebook,* edited by Ellen Cushman, Eugene R. Kintgen, Barry M. Kroll, and Mike Rose, 19–31. Boston: Bedford/ St. Martin's.

Pagnucci, Franco. 1998. *Ancient Moves*. Platteville, WI: Bur Oak Press, Inc.

Pagnucci, Gian S. 1989. *Application Processing*. Madison, WI: CUNA Mutual Insurance Group.

———. 1995. "Cyberwriting: A Story of Teaching, Learning, and Co-authoring." Doctoral dissertation. Madison, WI: University of Wisconsin.

———. 1997. "The TicToc Story." *Works and Days* 15: 45–61.

———. 1999. "TechJournals: Electronic Journal Keeping for the Technical Writing Classroom. In *The Journal Book for Teachers in Technical and Professional Programs*, edited by Susan Gardner and Toby Fulwiler, 106–18. Portsmouth, NH: Boynton/Cook.

Pagnucci, Gian S., and Dawn Abt-Perkins. 1992. "The Never Making Sense Story: Reassessing the Value of Narrative." *English Journal* 81: 54–58.

Pagnucci, Gian, and Edel Reilly. 2002. "Visions." *Acorn* 25 (4): 35.

Pagnucci, Gianfranco. 1979. *Face the Poem*. Platteville, WI: Bur Oak Press, Inc.

———. *Out Harmsen's Way*. Madison, WI: Fireweed.

Paley, Karen Surman. 2001. *I Writing: The Politics and Practice of Teaching First-Person Writing*. Carbondale, IL: Southern Illinois University Press.

Paley, Vivian. 1986. *Boys and Girls: Superheroes in the Doll Corner*. Chicago: University of Chicago Press.

———. 1990. *The Boy Who Would Be a Helicopter: The Uses of Storytelling in the Classroom*. Cambridge, MA: Harvard University Press.

Paradis, James. 1991. "Text and Action." In *Textual Dynamics of the Professions: Historical and Contemporary Studies of Writing in Professional Communities*, edited by Charles Bazerman and James Paradis, 256–78. Madison, WI: University of Wisconsin Press.

Pierce, Judy, Kay Terry, and Janice Ferguson. 1997. "Storytelling: An Effective Tool for Promoting Literacy and Language Development." *Ohio Reading Teacher* 31 (3): 67–68.

Postman, Neil. 1989. "Learning by Story." *The Atlantic* 264: 119–24.

Randall, Alice. 2001. *The Wind Done Gone*. Boston: Houghton Mifflin.

Rey, H. A. 1969. *Curious George*. Boston: Hougton Mifflin.

Ricoeur, Paul. 1984. *Time and Narrative: Volume I*. Chicago: University of Chicago Press.

Riessman, Catherine Kohler. 1993. *Narrative Analysis*. Newbury Park: Sage.

Robertson, Robbie. 1991. *Storyville*. Geffen Records.

Romano, Tom. 1995. *Writing with Passion: Life Stories, Multiple Genres*. Portsmouth, NH: Boynton/Cook.

Rose, Mike. 1989. *Lives on the Boundary: A Moving Account of the Struggles and Achievements of America's Educational Underclass*. New York: Penguin.

Rosen, Harold. 1984. *Stories and Meanings*. London: NATE.

———. 1986. "The Importance of Story." *Language Arts* 63 (Mar.): 226–37.

Rowling, J. K. 1997. *Harry Potter and the Sorcerer's Stone*. New York: Scholastic.

Schaafsma, David. 1989. "Gilbert's and Dave's Stories: Narrative and Knowing." *English Journal* 78: 89–91.

———. 1993. *Eating on the Street: Teaching Literacy in a Multicultural Society*. Pittsburgh: University of Pittsburgh Press.

———. 1999–2000. "Telling Stories, Drawing Maps." *Works and Days* 17–18 (33–36): 7–15.

Schank, Roger. 1990. *Tell Me a Story: A New Look at Real and Artificial Memory*. New York: Charles Scribner's Sons.

Schuster, Charles. 1990. "The Ideology of Illiteracy: A Bakhtinian Perspective." In *The Right to Literacy*, edited by Andrea A. Lunsford, Helene Moglen, and James Slevin, 225–32. New York: Modern Language Association.

Scott, Ridley. 1991. *Thelma and Louise*. Century City, CA: Metro-Goldwyn-Mayer Studios.

Sendak, Maurice. 1963. *Where the Wild Things Are*. New York: Scholastic.

Seuss, Dr. 1966. *The 500 Hats of Bartholomew Cubbins*. New York: Scholastic.

Shirley, John. 1986. "Freezone." In *Mirrorshades: The Cyberpunk Anthology*, edited by Bruce Sterling, 139–77. New York: Ace.

Silko, Leslie Marmon. 1977. *Ceremony.* New York: Penguin.

Shakespeare, William. 1986. *William Shakespeare: The Complete Works.* Compact Edition. Oxford: Clarendon Press.

Smith, Frank. 1982. *Understanding Reading: A Psycholinguistic Analysis of Reading and Learning to Read.* 3d Edition. New York: Holt, Rinehart, and Winston.

————. 1988. *Joining the Literacy Club.* Portsmouth, NH: Boynton/Cook.

Smith, Jeanne. 1994. "The Story's the Thing." In *Give a Listen. Stories of Storytelling in School,* edited by Ann M. Trousdale, Sue A. Woestehoff, and Marni Schwartz, 3–9. Urbana, IL: National Council of Teachers of English.

Spufford, Francis. 2002. *The Child That Books Built.* London: Faber and Faber.

Stafford, William. 1987. *An Oregon Message.* New York: Harper and Row.

Stone, Oliver. 1991. *The Doors.* Santa Monica, CA: Artisan Entertainment.

Tan, Amy. 1989. *The Joy Luck Club.* New York: Putnam's.

Tobin, Lad. 1997. "Reading and Writing About Death, Disease, and Dysfunction; or, How I've Spent My Summer Vacations." In *Narration as Knowledge: Tales of the Teaching Life,* edited by Joseph F. Trimmer, 71–83. Portsmouth, NH: Boynton/Cook.

Tolkien, John R. R. 1965. *The Fellowship of the Ring.* New York: Ballantine.

Trimmer, Joseph F. 1997. "Introduction." In *Narration as Knowledge. Tales of the Teaching Life,* edited by Joseph F. Trimmer, ix–xv. Portsmouth, NH: Boynton/Cook.

Trousdale, Ann M., Sue A. Woestehoff, and Marni Schwartz. 1994. *Give a Listen: Stories of Storytelling in School.* Urbana, IL: National Council of Teachers of English.

Twain, Mark. 1961. *The Adventures of Tom Sawyer.* New York: Holt, Rinehart and Winston.

Updike, John. 1960. *Rabbit, Run.* New York: Fawcrest.

Van Maanen, John. 1988. *Tales of the Field: On Writing Ethnography.* Chicago: University of Chicago Press.

Vielstimmig, Myka. 1999. "Petals on a Wet, Black Bough: Textuality, Collaboration, and the New Essay." In *Passions, Pedagogies, and Twenty-First-Century Technologies*, edited by Gail E. Hawisher and Cynthia L. Selfe, 89–114. Urbana, IL: National Council of Teachers of English.

———. 1999–2000. "From Hawaii to *Kairos*: Alt. Writing and the Ongoing Conversation." *Works and Days* 17–18 (33–36): 187–203.

Villanueva, Jr., Victor. 1993. *Bootstraps: From an American Academic of Color.* Urbana, IL: National Council of Teachers of English.

Volosinov, V. N. 1973. *Marxism and the Philosophy of Language*. Translated by Ladislav Matejka and I. R. Titunik. Cambridge, MA: Harvard University Press.

Vygotsky, Lev Semenovich. 1986. *Thought and Language.* Translated by Alex Kozulin. Cambridge, MA: MIT Press.

Wagner, Brandon. 2000. "Text of President-Elect Bush's Victory Speech Wednesday, as Released by the Bush Campaign." Accessed: 1 August 2003 at *http://brandon.wagner.home.mindspring.com/bush.htm*.

Warwick, Kevin. 2000. "Cyborg 1.0." *Wired* 8 (2): 1–4.

Winston, L. 1997. *Keepsakes: Using Family Stories in Elementary Classrooms.* Portsmouth, NH: Heinemann.

Witherell, Carol, and Nell Noddings. 1991. *Stories Lives Tell: Narrative and Dialogue in Education*. New York: Teachers College Press.

Wolff, Tobias. 1989. *The Barracks Thief: And Selected Stories*. New York: Bantam Doubleday Dell.

Yahoo! Movies. 2003. "All Time Box Office (U.S.)." Accessed 1 August 2003 at *http://movies.yahoo.com/boxoffice-alltime/rank.html*.

Author Index

Subject Index